The Actor's

Molière

Volume 2

THE DOCTOR IN SPITE OF HIMSELF

and

THE BOURGEOIS GENTLEMAN

in new translations by Albert Bermel

APPLAUSE
THEATRE BOOK PUBLISHERS
211 West 71 Street, New York, NY 10023

Printed in U.S.A.

ISBN O-936839-77-5

Library of Congress Cataloging-in-Publication Data

Molière, 1622–1673.
    The doctor in spite of himself.

    (The Actor's Molière ; v. 2)
    Translation of: Le médecin malgré lui, and Le bourgeois gentilhomme.
    1. Molière, 1622–1673—Translations, English.
I. Molière, 1622–1673. Bourgeois gentilhomme. English.
1987. II. Bermel, Albert. III. Title: Bourgeois gentleman.
V. Series: Molière, 1622–1673. Actor's Molière ; v. 2.
PQ1825.E5   1987   842'.4   87–1054
ISBN 0–936839–77–5

CONTENTS

Dedicated, with admiration and thanks, to Glenn Young

The Doctor in Spite of Himself

(Le Médecin malgré lui)

Sganarelle, a woodcutter
Martine, his wife
Monsieur Robert, his neighbor
Géronte, a landowner
Valère, servant of Géronte
Lucas, another servant of Géronte, Valère's uncle
Jacqueline, wife of Lucas
Lucinde, Géronte's daughter, in love with Léandre
Léandre, in love with Lucinde
Thibaut, a poor farmer
Perrin, his son

*Act I takes place in a forest clearing, in front of the house of
Sganarelle and Martine.   Act II takes place in Géronte's house.
Act III takes place outdoors, in front of Géronte's house.*

ACT ONE

A forest clearing. Before the house of Sganarelle and Martine.

They enter quarreling.

SGANARELLE No! I won't do it. And what I say goes. I'm the master here.

MARTINE You will do it. You may be the master but you'll do what I say.

SGANARELLE What is a wife? A sharp instrument for cutting a man down. Aristotle hit it when he said: Marry a woman, live with a demon.

MARTINE Listen to the clever man with his bonehead of an Aristotle.

SGANARELLE Clever is right. I knew my Latin grammar when I was a tot this high. And I spent six years carrying prescriptions for a top doctor. Find me one other woodcutter who has my powers of reasoning.

MARTINE I lost mine the day and the hour when I said, "I do."

SGANARELLE You lost more than that later. I curse the notary who invited me to sign my own downfall.

MARTINE Did you deserve to catch a woman like me?

SGANARELLE Admit it: you applauded my performance on our wedding night. You were lucky to find me.

MARTINE Lucky to find you! A slob who's pushing me into the poorhouse, a brute who eats up everything in the house!

SGANARELLE You're lying. Some of it I drink.

MARTINE Sells off our possessions, piece by piece!

SGANARELLE   Only the valuable stuff.

MARTINE   Even sold my bed out from under me!

SGANARELLE   Now you get up earlier.

MARTINE   Plus most of our furniture!

SGANARELLE   To make it easier when we have to move.

MARTINE   Gambles and boozes from morning to night!

SGANARELLE   Better than being idle.

MARTINE   And while all this goes on, what do you expect me to do with the children?

SGANARELLE   Anything you like.

MARTINE   I have those four little ones on my hands.

SGANARELLE   Let 'em drop.

MARTINE   They're always crying for a crumb to eat.

SGANARELLE   Give 'em a taste of the whip. Let them satisfy themselves by watching me eat. When I've had my fill of food and drink I want every member of my family to burp.

MARTINE   You drunken oaf, how long can we go on like this?

SGANARELLE   Wife, keep your voice down.

MARTINE   And how long do I have to put up with your bluster?

SGANARELLE   Wife, don't get carried away.

MARTINE   I'll teach you to shape up.

SGANARELLE   Wife, I have a warm temper and a woodcutter's arm.

MARTINE   Threats are cheap.

SGANARELLE   Wife, wife, your skin is itching.

MARTINE   Hooch hound!

SGANARELLE   Shall I tickle it with my stick?

MARTINE   Swill belly!

SGANARELLE   Shall I make you murmur in pain?

MARTINE   Gut rot!

SGANARELLE   Then hammer you into silence?

MARTINE   Big lip, double-crosser, chicken-heart, chiseler, sponger, gasbag, wastrel, worm, thief!

SGANARELLE   *(Beating her with his stick)*   So you enjoy punishment?

MARTINE   Stop, stop, stop, stop!

SGANARELLE   Isn't this the way to cool you off?

Enter Monsieur Robert.

MONSIEUR ROBERT   Hey, enough there! What's going on? A bully striking a woman like that?

MARTINE   I'm his wife.

MONSIEUR ROBERT   A disgrace!

MARTINE   *(Hands on hips)*   And if I want him to strike me?

MONSIEUR ROBERT   In that case, I'm all for it.

MARTINE   *(Driving him back step by step)*   Who asked you to interfere?

MONSIEUR ROBERT   My mistake.

MARTINE   Look at this busybody, trying to stop men from hitting their own wives!

MONSIEUR ROBERT   I take it back.

MARTINE   Is it any skin off your nose?

MONSIEUR ROBERT   Not a bit.

MARTINE   So why do you poke it where it doesn't belong?

MONSIEUR ROBERT   Never again, I promise.

MARTINE   Do I butt into your business?

MONSIEUR ROBERT   Not another word from me.

MARTINE   Maybe I like to be hit.

MONSIEUR ROBERT   That's your privilege.

MARTINE   It doesn't bruise you, does it?

MONSIEUR ROBERT   I'm leaving.

MARTINE   Don't come around here again with your bad manners.

She pursues him with a slap. He retreats toward Sganarelle, who drives him back in the opposite direction.

MONSIEUR ROBERT   I apologize, neighbor. Go ahead, hit your wife, give her the all-out treatment. I'll help, if you wish.

SGANARELLE   I don't wish.

MONSIEUR ROBERT   That's different, then.

SGANARELLE   When I want to beat her, I will; when I don't, I won't.

MONSIEUR ROBERT   It's up to you.

SGANARELLE   She's my wife, not yours.

MONSIEUR ROBERT   Looks like it.

SGANARELLE   I don't take orders from you.

MONSIEUR ROBERT   I'm not giving any.

SGANARELLE   I don't need your help.

MONSIEUR ROBERT   I withdraw it.

SGANARELLE   You've got some nerve, muscling in on other people's home lives. Take notice of the poet Cicero when he says, "Never come between a man and his missus." (*He pounds Monsieur Robert with his stick and chases him off, then returns to Martine, and tries to take her hand.*)   Now we'll make up. Shake on it.

MARTINE   Oh yes, after that rough a beating!

SGANARELLE   Forget it. Shake.

MARTINE   I won't.

SGANARELLE   You're not sore? Not my own little wifey?

MARTINE   Get away from me.

SGANARELLE   Come on, come on.

MARTINE   Not a hope.

SGANARELLE   What is it?

MARTINE   I want to stay mad.

SGANARELLE   Oh fiddle! For nothing?

MARTINE   You hit me too hard.

SGANARELLE   Well look, I'm sorry. Give me your hand.

MARTINE   I forgive you. But you won't touch me again till you make it up to me.

SGANARELLE   You're a silly girl to fret over a beating. These little things have to crop up now and then between partners. Five or six blows from me to you — they work up my desire. And energy . . . Now for the forest. Today I promise you at least a hundred bundles of wood. (*Exit.*)

MARTINE *(Alone)* Beast! I'll pay you back. A wife can always get even with her husband in a certain way, but that's not enough of a punishment for my stinker. I want some revenge that'll hurt him, and keep hurting.

Enter Valère and Lucas. Martine does not see them at first.

LUCAS We been sent out on a wicked hard consignment here, boy.

VALERE It may be worth the effort, uncle. Once the young mistress gets over her sickness, she'll marry. We ought to make money out of that. This fellow Horace stands a good chance with her, and he's free with his money. I know she likes the other one better, that Léandre, but the master will never have him for a son-in-law.

MARTINE *(Aside)* I need to come up with a neat trick, a surprise, so he'll never lay a finger on me again.

LUCAS The master may never get *no* son-in-law. The doctors are stumped.

VALERE We'll keep looking. Those are our orders. We could maybe find the answer in some out-of-the-way place like this.

MARTINE *(Aside)* Whatever it takes, whatever it takes! I'll fix him. With a stick. Like you use on a dog. That beating stung me to the heart. I can't get over it. *(Brooding, she turns and bumps into the two men.)* Oh, excuse me. Didn't see you there. I was taken up with my troubles.

VALERE We didn't see you, either.

LUCAS We was a bit taken up with our own troubles.

VALERE And we don't know these parts.

MARTINE Can I direct you?

VALERE Possibly. We'd like to locate some clever man, a doctor, a specialist who might have a remedy for our master's daughter. All of a sudden she contracted an illness and it took away her voice. The doctors have tried everything they know. We're looking all over. Sometimes you run into people here or there with secret cures. They know tricks the ordinary physicians never heard of.

MARTINE   Tricks!

VALERE   That's what we want — wonders, marvels!

MARTINE   *(Aside)* My luck has changed. Thank you, heaven! Here's the chance to get even with my stinker. *(Aloud)*   You came to the right place. We have a man here who's a miracle worker, especially with hopeless cases.

VALERE   Please, where can we find him?

MARTINE   Just over there among the trees. He's chopping wood.

LUCAS   A doc chopping wood?

VALERE   Don't you mean, picking herbs?

MARTINE   No, chopping wood is his hobby. He's a fantastic character. Eccentric. You'd never take him for what he is. He puts on wild clothes. Sometimes pretends he knows nothing. Keeps his wisdom bottled up inside. More than anything else he hates to practice his natural talent for medicine.

VALERE   These great men have their quirks, a dab of madness mixed in with their genius.

MARTINE   This one's madness is more than a dab. At times it takes over. It's like he's shifted character. So you have to beat the shift out of him. He'll never admit he's a doctor unless you both get sticks and belt him. Keep at it. At last he'll own up to what he'll surely hide at first. That's how we handle things here when we need him.

VALERE   Interesting. Weird. What's his name?

MARTINE   Sganarelle. You can't miss him. Look for a wide black beard, a ruff, and a yellow and green coat.

LUCAS   Yellow and green? Don't doctors wear black — y'know, in mourning for their patients?

VALERE   And he does real, honest miracles?

MARTINE   Listen. A woman here was given up by all the other doctors. They said she'd been dead for six hours. They were getting her shroud ready, fitting it on, when Sganarelle offered to help — after a cruel beating, of course. He took one look at her and dropped a dribble of liquid into her mouth. She got right up like she'd never had a thing the matter with her. And walked around the room the way I'm walking around you now.

VALERE   A wizard.

LUCAS   A devil.

VALERE   A devilish wizard.

MARTINE   Only three weeks ago a boy of twelve fell off the church steeple. Crash! He splattered his head, arms, and legs. They brought the bits of him home. Not a hope. Then they dragged in Sganarelle — after an unmerciful beating. He took out a secret salve — he makes it himself — and massaged the boy with it. The boy jumped up and ran outside to play marbles.

LUCAS   Ha! Marbles!

VALERE   A secret salve. I've heard of that. They call it wet gold.

MARTINE   That's the one, the cure-all.

LUCAS   Just what we need. Come, nephew, let's go beat him up.

VALERE   Madame, we thank you for this information.

MARTINE   Just remember my warning.

LUCAS   If all we got to do is clobber him good, trust us.

Exit Martine.

VALERE   Uncle, we're on to something at last.

Sganarelle comes into view, singing, with a bottle in his hand.

SGANARELLE Enough work for the time being. Let's take a breather. *(Drinks.)* Chopping dries out your salts. *(Singing)*

> They're so fine,
> my pretty bottle —
> they're so fine,
> the bubbles in your wine. . .
> All my pals would envy my
> fate if you were always full.
> But bottle, when I take a pull,
> why do you run dry?

(Speaking) Ah, fudge it, no point in getting morbid.

VALERE Yellow and green coat. Ruff.

LUCAS Black beard.

VALERE Let's look at him up close.

SGANARELLE Oh, my little honey bottle, how I love your little mouth! *(Sings again, but his voice trails off as he notices the two men.)*

> All my . . . pals would . . . envy my . . .
> fate if you were . . .

What the hell! Are those two out to get somebody?

VALERE He's the one. There's his axe.

LUCAS The spitting hemorrhage, just like she prescribed him.

SGANARELLE They're yacking and looking at me.

Valère and Lucas approach. Sganarelle puts down his bottle. Valère bows low. Sganarelle thinks he wants to swipe the bottle, and puts it on the other side of him. Lucas bows low. Sganarelle snatches up the bottle and hugs it.

Byplay, ad lib.

VALERE Monsieur, is your name Sganarelle?

SGANARELLE Yes and no. Depends on what you want.

VALERE We want to pay our compliments to a man called Sganarelle.

SGANARELLE   In that case, I am Sganarelle. Pay me? Compliment me? What for?

VALERE   Someone referred us to you. We're here to make a request.

SGANARELLE   If it's to do with my business, I'm at your disposal.

VALERE   You're most generous, monsieur. But please put your hat on again. We ought to take off ours, to you.

LUCAS   I would too, if I was wearing mine.

SGANARELLE   *(Aside)*   These people are plenty polite.

VALERE   We've been searching for you and nobody less. Great men are in great demand. We've heard of your gifts.

SGANARELLE   Everything you heard is true. I'm number one in the world when it comes to cutting wood.

VALERE   Ah, yes, but —

SGANARELLE   I spare no effort. I sweat out all my salts. You look at my finished work and you say: "There's nothing to say."

VALERE   That's not what we mean.

SGANARELLE   Better yet, I sell a bundle of one hundred for only one hundred ten sous.

VALERE   We're not interested in the price of wood.

SGANARELLE   I can't let 'em go for less, not with a wife and hungry children to support.

VALERE   Please! We know how things stand.

SGANARELLE   So does my price.

VALERE   Monsieur, you're joking when —

SGANARELLE   I am not joking. No discounts. No rebates.

VALERE   I'll try a different line. . .

SGANARELLE   Suit yourself. You might get it cheaper somewhere else. There's wood and there's wood. But mine is —

VALERE   All right, we'll drop this subject.

SGANARELLE   I take my oath, not one sou less.

VALERE   Let me —

SGANARELLE   No! In all conscience, that's below the going rate. I mean it sincerely. For this grade of long-burning —

VALERE   Monsieur, does a man of your reputation have to be so crudely evasive? Lowering yourself to talk this way! Why should a scholar, an eminent doctor like you, hide away here from the world's admiring eyes and bury his talents in the forest?

SGANARELLE   *(Aside)*   He's insane.

VALERE   Please don't try to mislead us any longer.

SGANARELLE   What?

LUCAS   Don't we know what we know? Cut out these wriggles and niggles and quibbles.

SGANARELLE   What do you want me to say? What do you take me for?

VALERE   What you are, a famous doctor.

SGANARELLE   Doctor yourself. I'm not and I never was.

VALERE   *(To Lucas)* Crazy. Just like she said. *(To Sganarelle)* Monsieur, we don't want to proceed to extreme measures.

SGANARELLE   Such as what?

VALERE   Certain actions we'd regret.

SGANARELLE   Damn it, you can proceed to anything you like. I'm not a doctor, and I don't see what you're getting at.

VALERE *(To Lucas)* We'll have to try the popular method. *(To Sganarelle)* Once again, monsieur, I ask you not to beat around the bush.

LUCAS Tell us straight out you're a doctor.

SGANARELLE *(Aside)* I'm getting hot. *(Aloud)* In two words that'll do for two thousand: I am *no doctor*.

VALERE Last warning. You're no doctor?

LUCAS You really ain't?

SGANARELLE I ain't.

VALERE Well, if you persist with this folly . . .

They beat him with sticks.

SGANARELLE Stop, stop, stop! I'm anything you say.

VALERE Monsieur, why did you drive us to this violence?

LUCAS We could strain our arms, no? We could injure you.

VALERE I'm truly sorry.

LUCAS I'm wore out.

SGANARELLE What the hell's going on? A gag of some kind? Are you both out of your skulls, trying to make me a doctor?

VALERE You won't give in? You still say you're not?

SGANARELLE I'm not. *(They beat him again.)* Stop, stop! All right, men, yes, I'm a doctor, a doctor, a surgeon — a leech even, if you want. I'll agree to anything, but stop battering me.

VALERE That's the way. I like you much better when you're reasonable.

LUCAS Then we don't have to kill ourselves hurting you.

VALERE You're a world-renowned physician, a miracle worker.

LUCAS   Is that something to be ashamed of?

SGANARELLE   *(Aside)*   What if I'm the one who's wrong? Did I become a doctor without noticing?

VALERE   I'm glad you finally leveled with us. You won't regret it. We're going to make it worth your while.

SGANARELLE   You couldn't have somehow slipped up? Taken me for someone else?

LUCAS   Wide black beard.

VALERE   Ruff. Yellow and green coat.

LUCAS   Name of Sganarelle.

VALERE   You're the cleverest doctor on earth.

SGANARELLE   I see.

LUCAS   You cured I don't know how many corpses.

SGANARELLE   Did I now?

VALERE   They thought this woman was dead for six hours. They were fitting her shroud and then, with one dribble of something on her tongue, you brought her back and she walked around the room, just like I'm walking around you.

SGANARELLE   Strike me dead!

LUCAS   A boy of twelve fell off a steeple, busted his head, arms, legs. Then you rubbed him down with some anecdote, and he stood up like new and ran out to play marbles.

SGANARELLE   Carry me off!

VALERE   So there it is. You'll do very nicely with us. Name your own fee and we'll take you with us.

SGANARELLE   Name my own fee?

VALERE   That's right.

SGANARELLE Now I remember. I am a doctor. How could I stupidly forget? What's next? Where do we go? How soon?

VALERE Come. You'll see a girl who lost her voice.

SGANARELLE Don't look at me. I didn't find it.

VALERE *(To Lucas)* He does have a sense of humor.

LUCAS I figured something like that.

VALERE Let's leave now.

SGANARELLE Without a doctor's gown? And hat?

VALERE We'll find them for you.

SGANARELLE *(Offering Valère his bottle)* Here, hold this. That's where I keep my magic cures. *(Turns to Lucas and spits on the ground.)* You, step on that. Doctor's orders.

LUCAS This is my kind of doctor. Bound to do well because he's a born joker.

ACT TWO

In Géronte's house.   Géronte, Valère, Lucas, Jacqueline.

VALERE Yes, you'll be delighted, master. He's the greatest doctor on earth.

LUCAS After they made him they threw away the mold, and the mildew. All the other doctors ain't fit to unlace his breeches.

VALERE He performs miracles.

LUCAS He repudiates the dead.

VALERE He's full of whimsy at times. His mind wanders off and he doesn't catch up with it.

LUCAS He loves to fool around. Now and then you might think someone had banged him over the head with an axe.

VALERE But inside he's all learning. He often drops profound remarks.

LUCAS When he wants, he can talk like he was spouting from the encyclopodium.

VALERE He already has an immense reputation here. Everyone's flocking to him.

GERONTE I'm dying to see him. Bring him in at once.

VALERE I'll get him. *(Exit.)*

JACQUELINE My land, master, this doctor'll do the same as the rest did. I say it'll be twelve of one and half a dozen of the other. You ask me, the best medicine you could give your girl'd be a nice-looking young husband she has some infection for.

GERONTE Nurse, you're very free with your advice.

LUCAS Dry up, Jacqueline. Nobody asked you to add your distribution.

JACQUELINE I say it and I resay it: All your doctors don't do no good. Your girl don't want no more rhubarb and senna and hot poultices. Give her a man of her own.

GERONTE She's in no state now, with this infirmity, to impose her on a healthy man. Besides, I did plan to marry her off, didn't I? And she opposed me, didn't she?

JACQUELINE Course she did. You told her to marry a man she didn't like. Why couldn't you pick that Léandre? She was fond of him. I bet he'll still take her. You ask him.

GERONTE Léandre's not right for her. He's not wealthy like Horace.

JACQUELINE   He's going to come in for a ton of money when his uncle dies.

GERONTE   Money to come is so much hot air. You must have money in your hands, not in your hopes. Pray all you want for him to die, but the angel of death doesn't always keep his ears open. You can grow long in the tooth waiting for somebody to die so that you can live well.

JACQUELINE   Me, I was always told happiness comes before money — in marriage and every other declivity. Fathers and mothers are always asking, "How much does he own?" or "What does she bring?" Old Man Pierre married his daughter to a crony who had an acre more vines than that youngster she was besmirched with. Now the poor girl's turned as yellow as a grapefruit, and the old buzzard's still alive, and all she's had out of the match is playing nursemaid and housemaid to a crock who's been dying for twenty years. We don't have long to enjoy ourselves on earth, master; and I'd sooner give my daughter a good, suitable husband than all the gold in Sodom and Gomorrah.

GERONTE   Damn it, nurse, you do chatter on! You get too worked up. You'll sour your milk.

LUCAS   Button your lip, you noisy shemale. *(Rapping Géronte on the chest for emphasis)* The master knows what he's up to. He doesn't need your affinities. Stop giving us pieces of your mind and stick to giving your baby the titty.

GERONTE   Take it easy! Hey! Easy there!

LUCAS   I just want to put her in her place, master, and keep her properly deformed.

GERONTE   You don't have to do it so forcefully.

Re-enter Valère, then Sganarelle who wears a black gown and a pointed hat.

VALERE   Brace yourself, master. Here's your doctor.

GERONTE   Welcome to my house, doctor. We need you desperately.

SGANARELLE   Hippocrates says . . . that we should both keep our hats on.

GERONTE   Hippocrates says that?

SGANARELLE   He does.

GERONTE   In what chapter?

SGANARELLE   His chapter on hats.

GERONTE   If Hippocrates says so . . .

SGANARELLE   Doctor, having heard of the marvelous things that you —

GERONTE   Excuse me, are you speaking to me?

SGANARELLE   Certainly.

GERONTE   I'm no doctor.

SGANARELLE   You're no doctor?

GERONTE   I'm really not.

SGANARELLE   *(Beating him with a stick)* You're sure?

GERONTE   Sure! Stop, stop, stop!

SGANARELLE   You are now. I never had any other training.

GERONTE   What kind of doctor have you found me?

VALERE   I warned you he was a funny case.

GERONTE   Is he? I'll soon send him packing. With his case.

LUCAS   Don't get yourself aggregated, master. It's all for a laugh.

GERONTE   I am not laughing.

SGANARELLE   Monsieur, I beg your pardon for the liberty I took.

GERONTE   At your service.

SGANARELLE   I'm desolated . . .

GERONTE   It's nothing.

SGANARELLE   . . . About those whacks and thumps . . .

GERONTE   They're all over now.

SGANARELLE   . . . That I had the honor of administering —

GERONTE   We'll say no more about them. Doctor, I have a daughter who's fallen into a strange sickness.

SGANARELLE   I couldn't be happier, monsieur, that your daughter needs me. I wish with all my heart that you needed me, too — you and your whole family — to demonstrate how eager I am to serve you.

GERONTE   I'm grateful for your kind wishes.

SGANARELLE   I mean them most sincerely.

GERONTE   I'm flattered.

SGANARELLE   What is your daughter's name?

GERONTE   Lucinde.   .

SGANARELLE   Lucinde! A lovely name to medicate: Lucinde!

GERONTE   I'll go see what she's doing.

SGANARELLE   And who's that sizable woman there?

GERONTE   My little one's milk nurse. *(Exit.)*

SGANARELLE   What a splendid specimen of milkiness! Oh, milk nurse, you tantalizing milk nurse, my doctorate is the humble slave of your milky abundance. What I'd only give to be the lucky brat who sucks the milk *(He touches her breast.)* of your human kindness. All my remediation, all my burning wisdom, my very professional touch — these are yours if —

LUCAS Hey, doctor, hands off my wife!

SGANARELLE Oh, she's your wife?

LUCAS Mother of my brood.

SGANARELLE You have a brood, too? I didn't realize. *(Holds out his arms to Lucas.)* But I'm glad to hear it because of my love for *(Hugging Jacqueline)* the two of you.

LUCAS *(Plucking him away)* Please, doctor, not so dispassionate.

SGANARELLE I'm truly tickled that you're a team. I congratulate her for having *(Goes to embrace Lucas again, ducks under his arms, and throws himself at Jacqueline's bosom.)* a man like you. And I congratulate you for having a woman who's this good-looking, good-natured, and upholstered.

LUCAS We don't need your conflagrations.

SGANARELLE Don't you want me to rejoice with you over such a beautiful union?

LUCAS With me, all you want.

SGANARELLE I'm equally interested in you both, and if I hug you to show my joy *(Same business as before.)* , I must for the same reason do it to her.

LUCAS *(Tugging once more)* Doctor, lay off her.

SGANARELLE I'll willingly lay off her.

Re-enter Géronte.

GERONTE Doctor, they're sending my daughter right in.

SGANARELLE I'm ready for her, monsieur, with all my medicine.

GERONTE Where is it?

SGANARELLE *(Tapping his forehead)* Up here.

GERONTE Very good.

SGANARELLE *(Trying to handle Jacqueline's breasts)* I'm trying to keep an eye on every member of your household. I must, as a priority, try your nurse's milk by paying a little visit to her breast.

LUCAS *(Tugging him away and spinning him into a pirouette)* Never! That's something I insolently tolerate.

SGANARELLE It's the doctor's duty to inspect the nurse's nipples.

LUCAS I can't possibly forbid it.

SGANARELLE You defy the doctor? Out of here!

LUCAS I perfidiously refuse.

SGANARELLE *(Looking at him askance)* I'll give you a fever.

JACQUELINE *(Tugging at Lucas and spinning him into a pirouette)* Out when he tells you! Don't you think I'm big enough to take care of myself if he tries anything underhanded?

LUCAS I don't like the way he relinquishes you.

SGANARELLE For shame! Jealous about his wife!

GERONTE Here's my daughter.

Enter Lucinde.

SGANARELLE She's the patient?

GERONTE Yes. I have only one child. I'd be stricken if she died.

SGANARELLE She's not allowed to without a doctor's prescription.

GERONTE A chair, here!

SGANARELLE For an invalid she's not all that repulsive. I'd say a healthy, strapping man could adapt to her.

GERONTE Doctor, you made her laugh!

SGANARELLE   When the patient laughs at the doctor, it's the most encouraging sign.   Well now, Lucinde, what's all this about? Where's the trouble?

LUCINDE   *(Pointing to her mouth, head, and chin)*   Han, hi, hom, han.

SGANARELLE   What was that again?

LUCINDE   *(Same gestures)*   Han, hi, hom, han, han, hi hom.

SGANARELLE   And again.

LUCINDE   Han, hi, hom.

SGANARELLE   Oh, you mean han, hi, hom, ha, ha?   I don't follow. What the hell language is that?

GERONTE   It's her sickness.   She's dumb.   Up to now nobody's been able to find out why.   Because of that we had to put off her marriage.

SGANARELLE   How come?

GERONTE   Her intended wants to wait till she's cured.

SGANARELLE   Who is this moron who doesn't want a dumb wife? I wish to God mine had the same complaint.   I'd take good care to keep her from being cured.

GERONTE   I beg you, doctor: do your utmost to rid her of this affliction.

SGANARELLE   I will, my very utmost.   Tell me, does it bother her much?

GERONTE   Yes.

SGANARELLE   Is she in pain?

GERONTE   Terrible pain.

SGANARELLE   That's great.   Does she go to the you know what?

GERONTE   Yes.

SGANARELLE   Generously?

GERONTE   I wouldn't know.

SGANARELLE   Does it look clear and sparkling?

GERONTE   I'm not up on these things.

SGANARELLE   Lucinde, give me your wrist. This pulse tells me that your daughter is dumb.

GERONTE   That's correct, doctor. You hit it right off.

SGANARELLE   Aha!

JACQUELINE   See how he disfigured what it was!

SGANARELLE   We physicians, you know, we spot these things without hesitating. A quack would have started stammering, "It's this or else that." Me, I put my finger on it and tell you straight out your daughter's dumb.

GERONTE   Yes, but can you tell me why?

SGANARELLE   Nothing's easier. She lost her voice.

GERONTE   But the cause, please. Why did she lose her voice?

SGANARELLE   All our leading authorities will instruct you that she has an impediment to the mobility of her tongue.

GERONTE   Then what's your professional diagnosis of this impediment to the mobility of her tongue?

SGANARELLE   On that very point Aristotle says . . . some really fine things.

GERONTE   I can imagine.

SGANARELLE   Ah, there was a great man!

GERONTE   Must have been.

SGANARELLE A *great* man. *(Displaying the length of his forearm.)* Greater than even I am by that much. Now, to come back to our diagnostic analysis. I hold that this impediment to the mobility of her tongue is caused by certain fluids, which we scholars call noxious humors. Noxious means . . . fluids or humors which are noxious. The vapors given off by the exhalations of influences that arise from the seat of the disease, spreading, in other words, by . . . Do you know Latin?

GERONTE None at all.

SGANARELLE *(Astonished)* You don't know Latin?

GERONTE No.

SGANARELLE *(To the accompaniment of comic gestures) Cabricias arci thuram, catalamus, singulariter, nominativo haec Musa* — the muse — *bonus bona bonum, Deus sanctus, estne oratio latinas? Etiam,* yes. *Quare,* why? *Quia substantivo et adjectivus concordat in generi, numerum, et casus.*

GERONTE Oh, why couldn't I have been a scholar?

JACQUELINE There's a clever man for you, an aficionado.

LUCAS Must be. I can't supersede one word.

SGANARELLE Yes, these vapors I alluded to travel from the left side, where the liver is, to the right, where you find the heart, and it transpires that the lungs, which in Latin we call *armyan,* being connected to the brain, which we call *nasmus,* by way of the *vena cava,* which in Hebrew we call *cubile,* encounter the aforesaid vapors in their path as they pour into the ventricles of the scapula; and because the aforesaid vapors — pay close attention to this sequence, if you will — because the aforesaid vapors have a malign character . . . Listen carefully, will you?

GERONTE Yes, yes . . .

SGANARELLE . . . Have a malign character, which is caused by . . . Please concentrate.

GERONTE I will.

SGANARELLE . . . Caused by the acidity and aridity of the humors engendered in the concavity of the diaphragm, it follows that these humors . . . *Ossabandus, nequeys, nequer, potarinum, quipsa milus.* And that is precisely why your daughter's dumb.

JACQUELINE Oh hubby, wasn't that detrimental?

LUCAS Wish I was as well hung as his tongue.

GERONTE It's not possible to improve on his diagnosis. There was only one statement that startled me: the positions of the liver and the heart. I thought you reversed them. The heart is on the left, no? And the liver on the right?

SGANARELLE They used to be. But we've changed all that. We now practice medicine by an entirely new method.

GERONTE That I didn't know. Excuse my ignorance.

SGANARELLE Don't mention it. No need for you to be advanced as we are.

GERONTE Of course not. But doctor, what do you think should be done for this ailment?

SGANARELLE What I think should be done?

GERONTE Yes.

SGANARELLE In my view you must put her back in bed and feed her on plenty of bread soaked in wine.

GERONTE Why that?

SGANARELLE Because compounding bread and wine induces a sympathetic virtue which promotes speech. It's the only nourishment you give parrots. They ingest that and they learn to talk.

GERONTE A discovery! What a great man! Quick, bread and wine galore!

SGANARELLE   I'll be back this evening to see how she's getting along. *(Lucas escorts Lucinde out. To Jacqueline:)* Hold it, you! Monsieur, I must brew one or two remedies for your wet-nurse.

JACQUELINE   Not for me. I'm in perfect shape.

SGANARELLE   That's what is wrong, nurse. Perfect health is dangerous. I won't harm you: a little gentle bleeding and a soothing infusion.

GERONTE   Doctor, I don't understand that. Why do you bleed somebody who's not ill?

SGANARELLE   Ill? That doesn't count, so long as the experiment works. Just as you drink to prevent thirst, so you bleed to prevent sickness.

JACQUELINE   *(Retreating)*   Not for me. I don't let no one fool around with my body.

SGANARELLE   You may resist my remedies now, milky lady, but before long we'll infuse you to your heart's content. *(Exit Jacqueline.)* Good day, monsieur.

GERONTE   One moment, please.

SGANARELLE   What do you want?

GERONTE   To give you your fee, doctor.

SGANARELLE   *(Sticking his hand out behind him, from under the cloak, as Géronte opens his purse)*   I will not take it.

GERONTE   Doctor . . .

SGANARELLE   No.

GERONTE   Please wait.

SGANARELLE   Not possible.

GERONTE   I beg of you.

SGANARELLE   Don't make fun of me.

GERONTE Here it is.

SGANARELLE Can't take it.

GERONTE You must.

SGANARELLE I never work for money.

GERONTE I'm sure of that.

SGANARELLE *(Taking the money)* It's not counterfeit?

GERONTE Oh no.

SGANARELLE Because I'm not one of your mercenary doctors.

GERONTE I can see.

SGANARELLE I don't look for financial gain.

GERONTE I didn't think so. *(Exit.)*

Enter Léandre.

SGANARELLE *(Checking the money)* Not bad at all. As long as—

LEANDRE Doctor, I've waited a long time to see you. I've come to implore your help.

SGANARELLE *(Taking his wrist)* A very feeble pulse.

LEANDRE I'm not sick, doctor.

SGANARELLE Why the devil didn't you say so? Before I gave you a free pulse-reading?

LEANDRE *(Rapidly)* To explain quickly: My name's Léandre and I'm in love with Lucinde whom you just saw and whose father dislikes me and won't allow me near her so I plead for your cooperation which will permit me to carry out a plan I've thought up because I must have a few words with her for the sake of my happiness that is for the sake of my life.

SGANARELLE *(Faking anger)* What do you take me for? How dare you ask me to collaborate in your clandestine love affair? An escapade of this sort would undermine my doctoral dignity.

LEANDRE Hush, doctor, don't make a din.

SGANARELLE *(Pushing him away)* I will if I wish. You have some nerve.

LEANDRE Quiet, doctor!

SGANARELLE Some blundering —

LEANDRE Please!

SGANARELLE I'll teach you I'm not that sort of doctor, and that it's an outragc for you to —

LEANDRE *(Holding out a purse)* Doctor!

SGANARELLE — To imagine you can *(Taking the purse)* . . . buy me. Of course, I don't mean you personally. You're a decent fellow and I'd be glad to do you a favor. But there are these brazen types lurking all over who come around taking people for what they're not; and you can understand how they put my back up.

LEANDRE I apologize for my presumption.

SGANARELLE No need to. What's the plan?

LEANDRE You must realize, doctor, that this sickness of hers is a pretense. Other doctors have argued it back and forth. They didn't hesitate over the cause. Some of them said it was the brain, others the bowels or the spleen or the liver. But the real cause is love. Lucinde is only acting sick, to escape from a marriage that was imposed on her. Listen, I don't want anybody to see us together. Let's leave. I'll tell you on the way what I'd like you to do.

SGANARELLE Monsieur, you have aroused my protective sympathy to fever pitch. I'll unleash all my medical knowledge. The patient will either croak or be yours.

ACT THREE

Outside Géronte's house. Sganarelle and Léandre.

LEANDRE I'd say I pass quite well for an apothecary. Her father's hardly ever seen me, so this coat and wig ought to be enough of a disguise.

SGANARELLE No question.

LEANDRE All I need now is five or six fancy medical terms to make it sound as if I know what I'm talking about.

SGANARELLE Strictly unnecessary. The coat will cover all doubts. I don't understand any more of this gobbledegook than you do.

LEANDRE What!

SGANARELLE Fact. I'll be damned if I know the first thing about medicine. You're all right, so I can trust you, just as you trusted me.

LEANDRE You mean, you're not actually a . . .

SGANARELLE That's it. They made a doctor out of me with a stick. I didn't set myself up as that sort of a know-it-all. I never got past sixth grade. I have no idea why they came up with this brain wave; but when I saw they were going to force me to become a doctor, I let it happen and kissed off the consequences. After that, you wouldn't believe how the story flew around. Everybody takes me for the big medical mind. People are coming at me from all angles. I may just stay in the profession for the rest of my life. It's the most satisfying trade you can find. Whether you cure or kill you always collect that fee. Nobody dumps on you for doing a shoddy job. Malpractice? You can rip and hack the material any way you want. A shoemaker knows that if he ruins a scrap of leather he'll foot the bill himself; but in this trade it won't set you back a penny if you ruin a human hide. When you slip up you're not to blame. It's the fault of the corpse. And best of all, the dead are the most honorable, discreet people in the world. They never complain about the doctors who did them in.

LEANDRE   Yes, the dead are very nice that way.

SGANARELLE   *(Noticing Thibaut and Perrin approaching)* These two look as if they want a consultation. Wait for me at the back of the garden.

Exit Léandre.   Enter Thibaut and Perrin.

THIBAUT   Doctor, me and my boy Perrin here, we been looking for you.

SGANARELLE   Something serious?

THIBAUT   His poor mother, name of Parrette, six months now she's been sick in bed.

SGANARELLE   *(Holding out his hand for money)*   What do you want me to do about it?

THIBAUT   Give us a bit of medicine.

SGANARELLE   First, I must know what is wrong with her.

THIBAUT   Dripsy, doctor.

PERRIN   Dropsy, doctor.

SGANARELLE   Make up your mind. Is it dripsy or dropsy?

THIBAUT   Yes. I mean, she's all like blooted out. They tell me she has gallons of fluid inside and she keeps making more of it, instead of blood, in her liver or kiddly or blooder — they all call it something different. Every day she gets a high fleever, with cramps and aches in her leg muffles. She coughs and chokes enough to make you ill just listening. Sometimes I think she's done for when she starts in with the quavers and conniptions. The apothecary in our village keeps giving her cures that don't cure. He's set me back over a dozen good gold crowns, what with his relaxatives, excuse my language, and the hyacinth water and minerals he made her swallow — all them lotions and potions for motions. But they didn't do her no more good, as we say, than flogging a dead hearse.

He wanted her to take some of that drug they call pneumatic wine,
but, tell you the truth, I was scared it might settle her hash because
they say these high-priced doctors are wiping out any number of
folks with that cosmetic.

PERRIN   Emetic.

THIBAUT   We're stumped, doctor. What do we do next?

SGANARELLE   I don't understand a word you say.

PERRIN   Doctor, our ma is sick, and here's two crowns we brung
you to give us a remedy.

SGANARELLE   Aha! You I understand. This young man speaks
clearly and offers me an intelligible explanation. You say your
mother is dropsical because her organs are manufacturing water
instead of blood? Her body is bloated? She's feverish, with aches
in her leg muscles? Sometimes she suffers from quivers and
convulsions, that is, fainting fits? Have I correctly interpreted the
symptoms?

PERRIN   Yes, doctor. That's it on the nose.

SGANARELLE   I understood you instantly. Your father doesn't
know what he's talking about. So now you are asking me for a
remedy?

PERRIN   Yes, doc.

SGANARELLE   The sort of remedy that will cure her?

PERRIN   That's the sort we're after.

SGANARELLE   Here's a morsel of chayze. Make her take it.

PERRIN   Cheese?

SGANARELLE   Yes, it's a fortified chayze. It contains gold, coral,
pearls, and many other priceless ingredients.

PERRIN   Doc, we're most grateful t'you. We'll give it to her.

SGANARELLE As soon as possible. Force it down, if you must.
It's foul to the taste. Good. Oh yes: if she dies, be sure to give her
a slap-up funeral.

*Exeunt Thibaut and Perrin. Enter Jacqueline and, trailing her,
Lucas, who conceals himself.*

SGANARELLE Aaah! The delectable milk nurse. Hail, nurse of
my heart! The sight of you is rhubarb, cassia, and senna to my
soul, purging it of its melancholy.

JACQUELINE Tickle my ears, doctor, all that eloquation! I don't
know one syllabus of your Latin.

SGANARELLE Grow sick, nurse, I entreat you, sick with love for
me. Enrapture me by letting me cure you to high heaven.

JACQUELINE Thanks, doctor, but right this moment I don't requite
any cures.

SGANARELLE How I pity you, sweet nurse, for having such a
burden, a jealous husband.

JACQUELINE What can I do? I'm being splurged for my sins. The
nanny goat must nibble the grass where she's tied.

SGANARELLE But what pasture! — a peasant like him who
watches over you all the time and won't let anybody innocently talk
to you!

JACQUELINE You haven't seen a thing yet. That's only a taste of
his sultry nature.

SGANARELLE Is it possible? Could a man be vile enough to illtreat
a milky creature like you? I can think of one person, overflowing
nurse, not far from where you're standing, who'd count himself
lucky if he merely kissed the tips of your tootsies. Why should a
woman who's so well-designed fall into the clutches of an animal, a
bear, a lout . . .? Forgive me, nursie, if I speak this candidly about
your husband.

JACQUELINE Doctor, I know all too well that he deserves those
epitaphs.

SGANARELLE You bet he does. He also deserves to have you plant a couple of conical forms on his forehead for even suspecting you.

JACQUELINE That's quite true. It might be good for him if I tumbled into temptation.

SGANARELLE I prescribe that you find some way to settle the score with him. I mean, find some man. Now, ravishingly pretty nurse, if I were lucky enough to *be* the chosen man . . .

He holds out his arms to Jacqueline. Lucas bobs up between them. They separate and go off swiftly to either side.

Enter Géronte.

GERONTE Lucas, have you seen our doctor?

LUCAS I sure have. With my missus.

GERONTE Where's he gone?

LUCAS Don't know, but I know where he's going when I catch up with him.

GERONTE See if you can find my daughter.

Exit Lucas, grumbling. Re-enter Sganarelle, with Léandre.

GERONTE Doctor! I was wondering where you were.

SGANARELLE In your courtyard, unloading an excess of milk. How's the patient?

GERONTE A little worse since your remedy.

SGANARELLE Good. That shows it's working.

GERONTE Yes, but while it's working I'm afraid she may die of it.

SGANARELLE Trust me. I have remedies that cure death and every other setback. I like to wait till I hear the last rattle.

GERONTE Who is this man you've brought?

SGANARELLE   He's the . . . (*Mimes an apothecary pumping an enema into a patient.*)

GERONTE   The what?

SGANARELLE   The one who . . . (*Mimes again.*)

GERONTE   Who what?

SGANARELLE   Who, you know. . . (*Mimes again.*)

GERONTE   I see.

SGANARELLE   Your daughter will need his ministrations.

Enter Jacqueline and Lucinde.

JACQUELINE   Your daughter, master: she wanted a walk and some air.

SGANARELLE   Exercise — capital! Here, apothecary, check her functions with scientific care. Very shortly I'll review her malady with you. (*He draws Géronte away to the side of the stage, puts an arm around his shoulders and his hand under Géronte's chin to turn his head away from Lucinde and Léandre. Géronte keeps trying to look, while Sganarelle keeps swiveling his head or blocking his view. Meanwhile he talks to keep Géronte occupied.*)

Monsieur, there is a vast and subtle rift between doctors over the question of whether women are easier to treat than men. Please listen; this is urgent. Some say no; others say yes. I myself say yes and no. Insofar as the incongruity of the opaque vapors clashing in a woman's normal sensibility can cause the affective side to overpower the cognitive, we perceive that the instability of her opinions depends on the oblique movement within the moon's orbit; and since the sun, which sheds its illumination on this, our global convexity, finds —

LUCINDE   No, my feelings will never change, never!

GERONTE   That was my daughter! She spoke! Oh miraculous remedy! Oh unexcelled doctor! What can I do to repay you for this blessing?

SGANARELLE *(Pacing and mopping his brow)* She was a hard nut to crack.

LUCINDE Yes, father, I have my voice back. And now I can tell you I'll have no husband but Léandre. It won't do you any good to think of foisting Horace on me.

GERONTE But —

LUCINDE Nothing can alter my decision.

GERONTE What —?

LUCINDE Don't try to sway me with your irrelevant talk.

GERONTE If —

LUCINDE All your harangues won't work.

GERONTE I —

LUCINDE On this question my mind is closed.

GERONTE Still —

LUCINDE No parental threats can force me to marry against my wishes.

GERONTE You —

LUCINDE Your shouting and ranting are hollow.

GERONTE It —

LUCINDE My love will never yield to this tyranny.

GERONTE There —

LUCINDE I'll enter a convent rather than marry a man I don't love.

GERONTE Yet —

LUCINDE *(Deafeningly)* No! No way! Nothing doing! You're wasting your time. I won't listen. And that is that!

GERONTE   Oh, that tidal wave of words. How do I fight back? Doctor, I beseech you: make her dumb again.

SGANARELLE   That I can't manage. My only suggestion, if you'll take it, is to make you deaf.

GERONTE   No thank you. So, Lucinde, you think —

LUCINDE   Enough! Don't smother me with reasons. They can't move me.

GERONTE   By this evening you shall be Horace's bride.

LUCINDE   I'll be death's bride first.

SGANARELLE   In heaven's name, stop! Let me treat this. She's in the grip of a common and recognizable disease. I know exactly how to proceed.

GERONTE   Is it possible, doctor, for you to cure even a diseased mind?

SGANARELLE   I have therapy for everything. This time we'll use our apothecary. A word with you, apothecary. You can see she's smitten with Léandre, against her father's will. There's no time to lose. The humors are bubbling. If we don't find a swift antidote she'll get worse. The most appropriate one I can think of, in capsule form, is a heavy stimulant of runforit, combined with the usual dosage of matrimonium. She may spit this mixture back at you, but you're good at your work and it's your responsibility to make her swallow it. Walk her around the garden at first to pacify the vapors while I speak to her father. Lose no time. The remedy, fast! The only remedy there is!

Exeunt Lucinde and Léandre.

GERONTE   What were those preparations you mentioned, doctor? I don't recall hearing the names before.

SGANARELLE   They're crisis medicine.

GERONTE   Did you ever see such defiance?

SGANARELLE   Daughters can be willful.

GERONTE   You wouldn't believe how she's stuck on this Léandre.

SGANARELLE   Young people, hot blood.

GERONTE   As soon as I noticed how passionate she was I locked
her indoors.

SGANARELLE   Well done.

GERONTE   And I made certain they couldn't get in touch.

SGANARELLE   Ah, wise!

GERONTE   If I let them get together they'd do something wild.

SGANARELLE   Very likely.

GERONTE   She might even have run away with him.

SGANARELLE   Sound thinking.

GERONTE   Someone warned me: he's doing everything he can to
reach her.

SGANARELLE   What a clown!

GERONTE   He's wasting his time.

SGANARELLE   Ha, ha.

GERONTE   I'll never let him see her.

SGANARELLE   He's not dealing with a fool. He hasn't got your
tricks up his sleeve. Smarter than you they don't come.

Enter Lucas.

LUCAS   Hell's bells and bobbins, master, a crisis.

SGANARELLE   Exactly.

LUCAS   Your daughter's decapitated with that apothecary, who was
Léandre, and your doctor here ran the operation.

GERONTE What! Cut my throat behind my back? Quick, the police! No, I'll go. Lucas, don't let him get away. Now traitor, I'll see you in court. *(Exit.)*

LUCAS This is it, doctor. They'll hang you good.

Enter Martine.

MARTINE Oh lord, I had such a time looking for this house. Hello! Have you heard anything about the doctor I put you on to?

LUCAS Waiting right here under this hat. To be hanged.

MARTINE What? My husband hanged? What did he do?

LUCAS Abdicated our master's daughter.

MARTINE Oh my dear husband, are they really going to hang you?

SGANARELLE Looks like it.

MARTINE And you'll die in public?

SGANARELLE Do I have a choice?

MARTINE I'd feel better if you had finished chopping up the wood.

SGANARELLE Move on. You're breaking my heart.

MARTINE I think I'll stay and keep up your spirits. I promise not to leave till I see you stop swinging.

SGANARELLE Ah. . .

Re-enter Géronte.

GERONTE The commissioner will be here directly. They'll put you away at my discretion.

SGANARELLE *(Hat in hand)* Couldn't we commute the sentence to a nice light whipping?

GERONTE Abduction is a capital offense. It's in the hands of the law now. But what's all this?

Re-enter Léandre and Lucinde.

LEANDRE Monsieur, allow me to introduce myself, Léandre, and to restore Lucinde to you. Our plan was to elope and marry, but we've given that up. We want to do the right thing. I don't wish to rob you of your daughter. I'll take her only with your consent. Let me add, monsieur, that I have just now received some letters from which I learn that my uncle has died and left me all his property.

GERONTE Léandre, I am most favorably impressed by your upright character. With the greatest joy in the world I give you my daughter.

SGANARELLE A narrow squeak for the medical profession!

MARTINE Now you won't be hanged, you can thank me that you're a doctor, because I was the one who qualified you.

SGANARELLE Yes, and also qualified me for the wrong end of a stick.

LEANDRE It turned out so cheerfully for all concerned that you shouldn't bear a grudge.

SGANARELLE So be it. I forgive you, wife, for the beatings. You did raise me to this exalted height. But from now on, prepare to show every ounce of respect due to a man of my standing, because the rage of a doctor can be more terrifying than you'd believe. And you'd better believe it.

The end of
The Doctor in Spite of Himself

The Bourgeois Gentleman

(Le Bourgeois gentilhomme)

with some lyrics added

Monsieur Jourdain, bourgeois
Madame Jourdain, his wife
Lucile, his daughter
Nicole, a servant
Cléonte, in love with Lucile
Covielle, Cléonte's valet
Dorante, a count, in love with Dorimène
Dorimène, a marquise
Music Teacher
Student of the Music Teacher
Dance Teacher
Fencing Teacher
Philosophy Teacher
Tailor
Apprentice Tailor
Lackeys, Singers, Instrumentalisis, Dancers, Cooks, Apprentice Tailors (all groups including men and women), and others who take part in the Interludes — as many as the stage can hold or the production can afford.

The play takes place in Monsieur Jourdain's drawing room in Paris.

PART ONE

Music Teacher, Dance Teacher, Singers, Dancers, Violinists.

MUSIC TEACHER *(To his singers)* In here, in this room. Wait there till he comes.

DANCE TEACHER *(To his dancers)* And you as well, on this side.

MUSIC TEACHER Where's my student-composer? Is it done?

STUDENT Yes.

MUSIC TEACHER Let me see . . . Good, very good.

DANCE TEACHER Something new?

MUSIC TEACHER Yes, it's the melody for a serenade I had him compose while our man is waking up.

DANCE TEACHER May I see it?

MUSIC TEACHER You'll hear it — when he comes.

DANCE TEACHER You and I have plenty to keep us busy.

MUSIC TEACHER We've found the patron we both needed. Our Monsieur Jourdain is the softest touch. Your dance and my music could use a world full of people like him.

DANCE TEACHER Not quite like him. I'd be happier if he had a keener appreciation of the things we do for him.

MUSIC TEACHER True, he doesn't properly appreciate them, but he pays beautifully. That's what our arts need the most.

DANCE TEACHER But I like my little share of glory. Applause stimulates me. It's agonizing to play to dummies and clods and hear their vulgar responses. There's pleasure in extending yourself for

people who can detect the subtleties, who give a knowing
welcome to the finer passages. Nothing repays our labors better
than that.

MUSIC TEACHER Agreed. But honeyed words won't keep you
alive. Pure praise requires something solid stirred in. The most
heartfelt applause is delivered not with two hands, but one. Our
man gets everything jumbled. He claps at the wrong moment and
for the wrong reason. But he has perception in his purse. His
compliments are worth their weight in gold.

DANCE TEACHER There's crude commonsense in what you say,
but money is such a sordid thing that a self-respecting artist
should never show it any affection.

MUSIC TEACHER I notice that when our man hands you your
money, you manage to accept it.

DANCE TEACHER And with a smile. But I only wish that, with
all his wealth, he also had a modicum of taste.

MUSIC TEACHER That's my wish, too. In the meantime, he'll
compensate for our other clients who do have taste. What they
praise, he'll pay for.

DANCE TEACHER At last: he's coming.

Enter Monsieur Jourdain, with two Lackeys.

MONSIEUR JORDAIN Well, teachers, what's up? Are you going to
show me your little buffoonery?

DANCE TEACHER Buffoonery?

MUSIC TEACHER Buffoonery!

MONSIEUR JORDAIN The you know, the what's its name... Your
latest number.

DANCE TEACHER Ah.

MUSIC TEACHER We're ready for you.

MONSIEUR JOURDAIN I got held up. Had to dress today like the quality people. My tailor sent me a pair of silk tights. Thought I'd never squeeze into them.

MUSIC TEACHER We wait at your pleasure, of course.

MONSIEUR JOURDAIN Don't leave, either of you, till they bring my suit. You must see me in it.

DANCE TEACHER Whatever you say.

MONSIEUR JOURDAIN I'm a fashion plate, head to toe.

MUSIC TEACHER We don't doubt it.

MONSIEUR JOURDAIN This Indian robe, I had it custom made.

DANCE TEACHER Stunning.

MONSIEUR JOURDAIN My tailor tells me the quality people are like this in the morning.

MUSIC TEACHER It suits you down to the ground.

MONSIEUR JOURDAIN Lackeys! My pair of lackeys!

FIRST LACKEY What do you wish, monsieur?

MONSIEUR JOURDAIN Not a thing. I wanted to make sure you can hear me. *(To the Teachers)* What do you think of their liveries?

DANCE TEACHER Exquisite.

Monsieur Jourdain opens his robe to show off his narrow breeches of red velvet and a green velvet jacket.

MONSIEUR JOURDAIN My casual morning wear for practicing my fencing in.

MUSIC TEACHER Very sharp.

MONSIEUR JOURDAIN Lackey!

FIRST LACKEY Monsieur?

MONSIEUR JOURDAIN   The other lackey.

SECOND LACKEY   Monsieur?

MONSIEUR JOURDAIN   Hold my robe. You think I still look good without it?

DANCE TEACHER   Couldn't be more dashing.

MONSIEUR JOURDAIN   Now let's take a peek at your stuff.

MUSIC TEACHER   First I want you to hear your serenade. This is the composer, one of my students, uncommonly gifted.

MONSIEUR JOURDAIN   You shouldn't have handed it down to a student. Are you too proud to do the job yourself?

MUSIC TEACHER   Don't get the wrong impression from the word "student." A composer of this caliber knows as much as the masters, and the melody's as fine as any ever written.

MONSIEUR JOURDAIN   Let me have my robe back: I'll hear better. Wait, I'll hear better yet without the robe. No, give me it again. That's best.

WOMAN SINGER
        I love you, Charles, I love you,
        I love you, love you, love you
        so much I ought to hate you,
        not date you, Charles, but hate you.
        I'll never, never, never —

MONSIEUR JOURDAIN   Whoa! Too gloomy. Puts a man to sleep. Couldn't you jolly it up here and there?

MUSIC TEACHER   The melody must conform with the lyric.

MONSIEUR JOURDAIN   I once learned a really cute song. How does it go?

DANCE TEACHER   No idea. Which one?

MONSIEUR JOURDAIN   Something about sheep.

DANCE TEACHER   Sheep!

MONSIEUR JOURDAIN   Yes. Ah, got it!   *(Sings)*
>When I first met my Lily
>I figured she was chilly
>and nervous as a lamb .
>But that was all a sham.
>When Lily came to know me
>she soon began to show me
>that chilly she was not,
>but man o man, red hot!

(Speaking)   Cute, no?

MUSIC TEACHER   Cute as they come.

DANCE TEACHER   And you sing it with ah, expression.

MONSIEUR JOURDAIN   That's without knowing music.

MUSIC TEACHER   You ought to study music, monsieur, as you do dance. The two arts go together.

DANCE TEACHER   Open your mind to the finer things.

MONSIEUR JOURDAIN   Do the quality people learn music?

MUSIC TEACHER   Invariably.

MONSIEUR JOURDAIN   Then I must. But where's the time? I have my fencing teacher with his lessons, and I hired a philosophy teacher who starts this morning.

MUSIC TEACHER   Philosophy is one thing, but music, monsieur, music . . .

DANCE TEACHER   Music and dance, music and dance. They're all you need.

MUSIC TEACHER   Without music a nation can't survive.

DANCE TEACHER   Without dance a man flounders.

MUSIC TEACHER   All the disturbances, the wars all over the world happen only because people haven't studied music.

DANCE TEACHER   All man's misfortunes, all the tragic setbacks in history, the failures of statesmen, the defeats of great commanders — they all come from one source: inability to dance.

MONSIEUR JOURDAIN   How's that?

MUSIC TEACHER   Isn't war caused by discords among people?

MONSIEUR JOURDAIN   True.

MUSIC TEACHER   If they studied music, wouldn't that bring them toward harmony?

MONSIEUR JOURDAIN   You're right.

DANCE TEACHER   When somebody commits a blunder, don't we say he made the wrong move?

MONSIEUR JOURDAIN   That's what we say.

DANCE TEACHER   What is behind that wrong move? Inability to dance.

MONSIEUR JOURDAIN   You're both right.

MUSIC TEACHER   Are you ready for our program?

MONSIEUR JOURDAIN   Curious as can be.

MUSIC TEACHER   First, my little experiment. It's inspired by . . . *(Announcing)* The Variety of Emotions in Music!

MONSIEUR JOURDAIN   Not hearts and flowers!

MUSIC TEACHER   What! You don't like hearts and flowers?

MONSIEUR JOURDAIN   Please spare me hearts and flowers.

MUSIC TEACHER   Wait till you hear this. *(To the singers)* Come forward.

SOPRANO
> Why did you capture my heart with flowers?
> Why did you trap my poor heart under towers

of crocuses, roses, and poppies and posies,
of pansies and all kinds of other sweet fancies —
begonias, petunias, and lilacs and violets
and big yellow daisies with little black eyelets...

TENOR

Stop, stop! Give me a kiss!
Give me a lilting wet smack
that'll tilt me —

BARITONE

Give him a miss! Give him the shove!

SOPRANO

Orchids and peonies and asters and stuff,
Flowers I love —

TENOR

Give me that heat!
My heart is stopping. Let yours make it start.
Let them in unison quiver and thump!

BARITONE

Give him the bird! Give him the bump!

TENOR

Warmth delicious!

SOPRANO

Floral treasures!

BARITONE

She's capricious.

TENOR

She's so precious!

BARITONE

I'm so jealous!

SOPRANO

How I prize him!

BARITONE

I despise him.

SOPRANO
> Stop it, fellows!
> Peonies and soft poinsettias ...

TENOR
> Darling, let us —

SOPRANO
> Rhododendrons, blue hydrangea ...

BARITONE
> Why do you treat me like a stranger?

TENOR
> Face the danger!

BARITONE
> Can't I change her?

SOPRANO
> Marigolds and mums and jonquil ...

TENOR
> May we be forever tronquil!
> Give me loving —

BARITONE
> Give him nothing!

SOPRANO and TENOR
> Flowers' names are so euphonious
> that they make our hearts harmonious.

BARITONE
> Mine's the loneliest
> and the groaniest.

MONSIEUR JOURDAIN Is that it?

MUSIC TEACHER Rapturous!

MONSIEUR JOURDAIN It didn't rapture me. Not bad workmanship, though. The woman has decent ankles.

DANCE TEACHER   And now for my little something. A tribute to some of the loveliest movements and poses in. . . *(Announcing)* Variations on the Dance!

MONSIEUR JOURDAIN   No more flowers! No more hearts!

DANCE TEACHER   They're anti-flowers, anti-hearts, whatever you wish. Ready!

The Dancers perform the movements and steps choreographed and conducted by the Dance Teacher. This dance episode marks the end of the first act and forms the first interlude.

MONSIEUR JOURDAIN   That wasn't all terrible. I liked some. I forget which.

MUSIC TEACHER   It'll have more strength when we add music.

MONSIEUR JOURDAIN   I'm setting up this thing to please a lady who's coming to lunch, a real marquise.

DANCE TEACHER   We'll remain at your service.

MUSIC TEACHER   A man with your aspirations, monsieur, should sponsor a concert at home every Wednesday or Thursday.

MONSIEUR JOURDAIN   Do the quality people do that?

MUSIC TEACHER   Inevitably.

MONSIEUR JOURDAIN   It'll knock her out, won't it?

MUSIC TEACHER   It will impress her formidably. You'll want three voices — soprano, counter-tenor, and basso — accompanied by a cello, a lute, and a harpsichord for the continuos, plus two violins for the ritornellos.

MONSIEUR JOURDAIN   We ought to get a ukulele in there. The uke is my favorite instrument, and it blends in.

MUSIC TEACHER   Ah, leave these things to us.

MONSIEUR JOURDAIN   Don't forget to send your people at lunch time to give us those variations on the whatsits.

MUSIC TEACHER   You'll be gratified. I'm sure you'll enjoy the minuets.

MONSIEUR JOURDAIN   Minuets! The minuet's my dance. You must watch me minuet. Teacher, let's do it.

DANCE TEACHER   Your hat, monsieur. *(They salute each other with their hats, and the Dance Teacher sings the melody.)*
            La, la, la. La, la, la, la, la, la.
            Again! La, la, la. La, la. Keep the tempo,
            if you please. . .
            La, la, la. Hold that leg
            nice and firm.
            La, la, la. Don't roll shoulders
            around so much.
            La, la, la. La, la, la, la, la, la.
            Those twisted arms —
            are they deformed?
            La, la, la, la, la. Head up straight
            and feet turned out,
            but not like a penguin. La, la, la.
            Stand erect!

MONSIEUR JOURDAIN   *(Panting)* Uh?

MUSIC TEACHER   Finest demonstration I ever saw.

MONSIEUR JOURDAIN   While I think of it, how do you greet a real marquise?

DANCE TEACHER   You want to greet a marquise? But not a comtesse?

MONSIEUR JOURDAIN   A real marquise. Her name is Dorimène.

DANCE TEACHER   To display lavish respect, you step back, so, as you bow, then go toward her with three more bows, so, and on the third bow you stoop all the way to her knees, so.

MONSIEUR JOURDAIN   *(Imitating him)* Got it.

FIRST LACKEY   Monsieur, your fencing teacher is outside.

MONSIEUR JOURDAIN Send him in. This is something you two have to see.

Enter the Fencing Teacher. He hands Monsieur Jourdain a foil.

FENCING TEACHER Come, monsieur, the salute. Upright bearing. Some weight on the left thigh. Legs not so spread apart. Feet in line. Wrist lined up with the hip. Point of the weapon at shoulder height. Less extension of the arm. Left hand at eye level. Left shoulder further back. Head up. Aggressive stare. Advance! The trunk steady. Touch my foil in quart, and press forward. One, two. Back to position. Another thrust with feet in place. Spring back. When you attack, monsieur, the foil leads the way, body remains covered. One, two. Touch my foil in tierce, and press forward. Advance! The trunk motionless. Advance again. Thrust from there. One, two. Back to position. Another attack. Spring back. Parry, monsieur, parry! *(The Fencing Teacher scores several hits.)*

MONSIEUR JOURDAIN Uh?

MUSIC TEACHER You're doing marvelous things.

FENCING TEACHER I've repeatedly told you the secret of swordsmanship. Two principles: You give and you don't receive. It's impossible for you to receive if you deflect your opponent's foil from the direction of your body; and this is achieved with a flick of the wrist, either in or out.

MONSIEUR JOURDAIN And that's how a man who's no killer can kill his man without being killed?

FENCING TEACHER Precisely. You saw the demonstration?

MONSIEUR JOURDAIN Yes.

FENCING TEACHER This proves that the study of armed self-defense overshadows all the worthless studies like dancing and music and —

DANCE TEACHER Steady there, steel-slapper. Show respect when you mention dancing.

MUSIC TEACHER And even more when you mention music.

FENCING TEACHER   Who are these clowns, trying to compare their studies with mine?

MUSIC TEACHER   Look at him for a puffed-up freak.

DANCE TEACHER   Behind all that padding.

FENCING TEACHER   Little clodhopper! I could teach you a step or two. And you, little sour notes, I'll make you sing at the top of your voice.

DANCE TEACHER   And you, you great pincushion, I'll stick you a fast one.

MONSIEUR JOURDAIN   *(To Dance Teacher)*   Are you insane? Don't pick a fight with him. He knows all about tierce and quart. He can kill a person with logical demonstration.

DANCE TEACHER   I don't give a shot for his logical demonstration. Or his tierce and quart.

MONSIEUR JOURDAIN   Please don't incense him.

FENCING TEACHER   What! You squirt!

MONSIEUR JOURDAIN   Teacher, please.

DANCE TEACHER   Some fencer. He lumbers around like an elephant.

MONSIEUR JOURDAIN   Teacher, please.

FENCING TEACHER   Once I start in on you —

MONSIEUR JOURDAIN   Easy, easy!

DANCE TEACHER   Once I get my hands on your —

MONSIEUR JOURDAIN   Calm down, all you teachers.

FENCING TEACHER   I'll puncture your paper skin.

MONSIEUR JOURDAIN   For God's sake!

DANCE TEACHER   I'll dance all over your wooden head.

MONSIEUR JOURDAIN   For my sake!

MUSIC TEACHER   I'll blow a ton of brass down his epiglottis.

MONSIEUR JOURDAIN   For everybody's sake, stop!

Enter the Philosophy Teacher.

MONSIEUR JOURDAIN   My philosopher! Just in time. Here, teacher, work some philosophy. Make these characters declare peace on one another.

PHILOSOPHY TEACHER   What is the trouble, good people?

MONSIEUR JOURDAIN   They went wild over which of their professions is tops. They want to fight it out.

PHILOSOPHY TEACHER   Now, now, is that necessary? Haven't you read Seneca's essay on anger? Passion brings a man down to the level of a beast of prey. Must our instincts not be mastered by reason?

DANCE TEACHER   This ox badmouthed us both.

PHILOSOPHY TEACHER   A wise person rises above insults. Remain cool and patient.

FENCING TEACHER   These ninnies had the gall to compare their haphazard trades to my scientific profession.

PHILOSOPHY TEACHER   And should that bother you? What makes each of us distinctive is his wisdom and integrity.

DANCE TEACHER   I still say it's not possible to speak too highly of the knowledge of dance.

MUSIC TEACHER   The knowledge of music has been revered through the ages.

FENCING TEACHER   Armed self-defense is the most skillful, the most indispensable of all the branches of knowledge.

PHILOSOPHY TEACHER And where does that leave philosophy? The three of you have some nerve. Knowledge! Your practices are all pitiful, mindless hobbies. A gladiator, a street warbler, and a bobbing toad!

FENCING TEACHER You boring bow-wow!

MUSIC TEACHER Gassy pedant!

DANCE TEACHER Grunting prig!

PHILOSOPHY TEACHER Why, you urchins, you deadheads . . .

He hurls himself at them, and all three whale away at him.

MONSIEUR JOURDAIN Monsieur Philosopher!

PHILOSOPHY TEACHER Crooks, dolts, and braggarts!

MONSIEUR JOURDAIN Monsieur Philosopher!

FENCING TEACHER Cut him to shreds!

MONSIEUR JOURDAIN Teachers!

PHILOSOPHY TEACHER Pretenders!

MONSIEUR JOURDAIN Monsieur Philosopher!

DANCE TEACHER Step in his mouth!

MONSIEUR JOURDAIN Teachers!

PHILOSOPHY TEACHER Flimflammers!

MONSIEUR JOURDAIN Monsieur Philosopher!

MUSIC TEACHER Hammer his hide!

MONSIEUR JOURDAIN Teachers!

PHILOSOPHY TEACHER Weasels, insects, treacherous impostors!

Exeunt all four teachers, scrapping.

MONSIEUR JOURDAIN Monsieur Philosopher, Teachers, Philosopher, Teachers. . . Go on, then, and pound away all you want. I won't butt in. I might damage my robe.

Re-enter the Philosophy Teacher, straightening his collar.

PHILOSOPHY TEACHER Let's get on with our lesson.

MONSIEUR JOURDAIN I'm sorry about the beating you took from them.

PHILOSOPHY TEACHER It was nothing. One learns how to accept these incidents philosophically. *(Thundering)* I'll satirize them in the style of Juvenal and destroy them! *(Affably)* Forget about that. What do you want to study?

MONSIEUR JOURDAIN Everything. I have this tremendous hunger for learning. I'm furious at my parents for not forcing me to study when I was young.

PHILOSOPHY TEACHER *Nam sine doctrina vita est quasi mortis imago.* You understand that? Of course, you know Latin.

MONSIEUR JOURDAIN Yes, but make believe I don't.

PHILOSOPHY TEACHER It means, "Without knowledge life is hardly more than a reflection of death."

MONSIEUR JOURDAIN Great stuff, that Latin.

PHILOSOPHY TEACHER Where would you like to begin?

MONSIEUR JOURDAIN Wherever you say.

PHILOSOPHY TEACHER
>   Shall I teach you how to reason?

MONSIEUR JOURDAIN
>   What's the use of that?
>   How can I be smart and pleasing
>   when I meet an aristocrat?

PHILOSOPHY TEACHER
>   Logic is a lovely study:

Three main functions of the mind —
generalizing, categorizing, memorizing intertwined.

MONSIEUR JOURDAIN
No, that sounds too fuddy-duddy.
Dream up something more appealing.

PHILOSOPHY TEACHER
Ethics, then, is quite revealing.

MONSIEUR JOURDAIN
Ethics? Oh. Are they gallant?

PHILOSOPHY TEACHER
Ethics disciplines your feeling —

MONSIEUR JOURDAIN
Not for me. I like to rant.

PHILOSOPHY TEACHER
Physics could give pleasure to you.

MONSIEUR JOURDAIN
Physics? Don't they go right through you?

PHILOSOPHY TEACHER
Physics — properties of stones,
metals, minerals, sticks and bones,
hailstorms, comets, lightning, snow,
how the mountain ranges grow,
what propels a shooting star —

MONSIEUR JOURDAIN
No, that's too much brouhaha.
Give me something not so wet.
Why not teach me etiquette?

PHILOSOPHY TEACHER
I know what — we'll tackle spelling.

MONSIEUR JOURDAIN
Pardon me, monsieur, you're yelling.
Simply tell me what to do.

PHILOSOPHY TEACHER
    Start with A, E, I, O, U.

MONSIEUR JOURDAIN
    A, E, was it?

PHILOSOPHY TEACHER
    I, O, U.
    Vowels or vocal sounds.

MONSIEUR JOURDAIN
    That's new!

PHILOSOPHY TEACHER   The vocal sound A is formed with the mouth wide open: A.

MONSIEUR JOURDAIN A, A. Yes.

PHILOSOPHY TEACHER   The vocal sound E brings the jaws closer and stretches the corners of the mouth toward the ears: A, E.

MONSIEUR JOURDAIN A, E. A, E. So it does. Beautiful.

PHILOSOPHY TEACHER   And the vocal sound I relaxes the edges of the mouth and further separates the upper from the lower jaw: A, E, I.

MONSIEUR JOURDAIN A, E, I. I, I, I. It's true! Up with learning!

PHILOSOPHY TEACHER   The vocal sound O is formed by opening the jaws more yet and closing off the lips, upper and lower, at the corners: O.

MONSIEUR JOURDAIN O, O. Couldn't go better. A, E, I, O. I, O. Fascinating. I, O. I, O.

PHILOSOPHY TEACHER   You shape your mouth in a little circle which is itself an O.

MONSIEUR JOURDAIN O, O, O, O. I do too. O. It's so reassuring to know something.

PHILOSOPHY TEACHER   The vocal sound U is formed by almost closing the teeth and protruding the lips: U.

MONSIEUR JOURDAIN   U, U.   By God, it's true.   U.

PHILOSOPHY TEACHER   You push your lips forward as if you were sulking.   That's why, when you want to jeer at someone, you simply say, "O, U."

MONSIEUR JOURDAIN   O, U.   That's it.   Why didn't my parents force me to learn all this long ago?

PHILOSOPHY TEACHER   Tomorrow we'll look at the other letters, the consonants.

MONSIEUR JOURDAIN   Are they as interesting as these?

PHILOSOPHY TEACHER   They are at least equally consequential. Take the consonant D.   You pronounce it by pressing the tip of the tongue against the palate behind the upper teeth.   Da.

MONSIEUR JOURDAIN   Da, da.   Yes!   Da, da.   Oh father, oh mother, I've got it in for you now!

PHILOSOPHY TEACHER   For the consonant F you rest the teeth briefly on the lower lip.   Fa.

MONSIEUR JOURDAIN   Fa, fa.   More truth, more beauty.

PHILOSOPHY TEACHER   For R, you curl the tip of the tongue against the palate, so that it momentarily gives way before the force of the breath, and then returns to the same position, trembling. Rra.

MONSIEUR JOURDAIN   R, R, Ra.   R, R, R, R, R, Ra!   There it is. You're a giant brain, teacher.   But me — I've wasted all these years. R, R, R, Ra!

PHILOSOPHY TEACHER   I will go on to explain these wonders in depth.

MONSIEUR JOURDAIN   Please do.   And now — I must let you in on a secret.   I'm in love with one of the quality people, and I'd like your help in writing a little message I can drop at her feet.

PHILOSOPHY TEACHER   Why not?   Do you want to compose it in verse?

MONSIEUR JOURDAIN   No, no. No verse.

PHILOSOPHY TEACHER   Oh, you want it in prose.

MONSIEUR JOURDAIN   No. Not in prose, not in verse.

PHILOSOPHY TEACHER   It must be one or the other.

MONSIEUR JOURDAIN   Why?

PHILOSOPHY TEACHER   Monsieur, there are only two ways to express yourself: in prose or in verse.

MONSIEUR JOURDAIN   That's the only choice?

PHILOSOPHY TEACHER   Correct. Everything that's not prose is verse, and everything that's not verse is prose.

MONSIEUR JOURDAIN   What is it, then, when we talk?

PHILOSOPHY TEACHER   Prose.

MONSIEUR JOURDAIN   Fact? When I say, "Nicole, bring my slippers and nightcap," that's prose?

PHILOSOPHY TEACHER   It is.

MONSIEUR JOURDAIN   What a discovery! I've been speaking prose for more than forty years and never knew it. I'm forever in your debt for teaching me that. So, here's what I want the message to state: "Fair marquise, your beautiful eyes make me die of love." Only I want to put it in the gallant style.

PHILOSOPHY TEACHER   Say that the flames from her eyes shrivel your heart to ashes, that for her you suffer night and day the tortures of the da —

MONSIEUR JOURDAIN   No, no, no. I don't need all that. Just what I said: "Fair marquise, your beautiful eyes make me die of love."

PHILOSOPHY TEACHER   You ought to open it up a little.

MONSIEUR JOURDAIN   No, those are the only words in the
message, but arrange them fashionably, the way they ought to go.

PHILOSOPHY TEACHER   First, you could try what you said. Or
there's, "Of love die me make, fair marquise, your beautiful eyes."
Or, "Your beautiful eyes of love me make, fair marquise, die." Or,
"Die your beautiful eyes, fair marquise, of love me make." Or even,
"Me make your beautiful eyes die, fair marquise, of love."

MONSIEUR JOURDAIN   Which of those is best?

PHILOSOPHY TEACHER   The one you said: "Fair marquise, your
beautiful eyes make me die of love."

MONSIEUR JOURDAIN   I never took lessons, yet I got it right first
time. My heartiest thanks. Please be here early tomorrow.

PHILOSOPHY TEACHER   Without fail. *(Exit.)*

MONSIEUR JOURDAIN   My suit! What, it's not here yet?

SECOND LACKEY   No, monsieur.

MONSIEUR JOURDAIN   That tailor keeps me waiting on a day when
I'm swamped with business appointments. Infuriating! A four-day
flu on him! If I had him here in my hands, that despicable, disloyal
dog of a tailor, that son of a stitch, I'd — *(Enter the Tailor.)*
You're here! I was about to get annoyed with you.

TAILOR   I couldn't make it earlier. I've had twenty apprentices
slaving over your suit.

MONSIEUR JOURDAIN   The silk tights you sent me were so narrow
they already have two seams busted.

TAILOR   They'll stretch to size, and more.

MONSIEUR JOURDAIN   Yes, if I split 'em wide open. And those
shoes you had made for me, they pinch like fury.

TAILOR   They don't.

MONSIEUR JOURDAIN   What do you mean, don't?

TAILOR   They don't pinch.

MONSIEUR JOURDAIN   I say they do. They pinch!

TAILOR   Monsieur, you imagine it.

MONSIEUR JOURDAIN   I imagine it because —

TAILOR   Now, this will be the most colorful suit in the whole Court. It's a masterpiece, formal wear that is not black.

MONSIEUR JOURDAIN   But look at this: you got the flowers wrong side up.

TAILOR   Everybody who's anybody wears them this way.

MONSIEUR JOURDAIN   The quality people have their flowers wrong side up?

TAILOR   Naturally.

MONSIEUR JOURDAIN   In that case —

TAILOR   If you prefer, I'll switch them around.

MONSIEUR JOURDAIN   No, no. You think that suit will look all right on me?

TAILOR   I defy any artist to paint something that is more *you*. The man in my workshop who does culottes is the world's supreme creative genius, and another is the hero of our time when it comes to fitting doublets.

MONSIEUR JOURDAIN   Are the wig and plumes correct?

TAILOR   Everything is *comme il faut*.

MONSIEUR JOURDAIN   Aha, tailor man, I see you wearing some fabric from the last suit you made me. I remember that material.

TAILOR   It looked so winning I decided on an extra suit out of it for myself.

MONSIEUR JOURDAIN   From my fabric? I ought to —

TAILOR   Wouldn't you like to try the suit on?

MONSIEUR JOURDAIN   Yes, hand it over.

TAILOR   That's not how we do things. My people will dress you to music. Hey, you!   Put this suit on monsieur the way we do it for the quality.

The Tailor's Apprentices enter. They remove Monsieur Jourdain's fencing breeches and jacket. They put on his new suit. He parades among them, in time to music.

APPRENTICE   Your honor, please remember a little something for the apprentices.

MONSIEUR JOURDAIN   What did you call me?

APPRENTICE   Your honor.

MONSIEUR JOURDAIN   Your honor!   That's what you hear when they take you for a quality person. Dress like a middle-class nobody, a bourgeois, and see how many "your honor's" you collect. Here, this is for "your honor."

APPRENTICE   We're most grateful, my lord.

MONSIEUR JOURDAIN   My lord! Wait, young man, "my lord" deserves an extra thought. It's not a mean title, my lord. Here's your gift from my lord.

APPRENTICE   After this, we'll drink a toast to your grace.

MONSIEUR JOURDAIN   My grace? Wait, don't go yet. Your grace — to me! There. That's for "your grace."   If he goes up to "your majesty" he'll have the whole purse.

APPRENTICE   Our profound and lasting thanks, your maj—

Monsieur Jourdain stops the Apprentice's mouth with one hand and holds on to his purse with the other.

The Apprentices express their delight with a dance, which closes the second act and forms the second interlude.

MONSIEUR JOURDAIN Lackeys, get behind me. I'm about to let everyone in town see my suit. Stay right on my heels — it's important — so people know you're mine.

LACKEYS Very good, monsieur.

MONSIEUR JOURDAIN First, call Nicole. I have some instructions for her. Stay! There she is.

Enter Nicole.

MONSIEUR JOURDAIN Nicole!

NICOLE Yes?

MONSIEUR JOURDAIN Pay attention now —

NICOLE Ha ha ha ha ha. . .!

MONSIEUR JOURDAIN What's the joke?

NICOLE Ha ha ha ha ha . . .!

MONSIEUR JOURDAIN Stupid girl. What's she snickering for?

NICOLE Ha ha ha — the way you're dolled up — ha ha ha!

MONSIEUR JOURDAIN So?

NICOLE Oh save me, it hurts . . . ha ha ha ha ha. . .!

MONSIEUR JOURDAIN The minx! Is she laughing at me?

NICOLE Never, master, I wouldn't dream of ha ha ha ha ha. . . !

MONSIEUR JOURDAIN You let out one more laugh and I'll dent your nose.

NICOLE Sorry, master, but you're such a ha ha ha ha. . .! I can't hold it ba-ha-ha-ha-hack. Ha ha ha ha.

MONSIEUR JOURDAIN I'll —

NICOLE Excuse me. Ha ha ha ha ha. . .!

MONSIEUR JOURDAIN This is it! One more laugh and I'll crack you across the chops.

NICOLE That's better, master. You did it. No more laughs.

MONSIEUR JOURDAIN Better not be. You have to —

NICOLE Ha ha ha ha ha. . .!

MONSIEUR JOURDAIN While I'm out, clean up and straighten the—

NICOLE Ha ha ha ha ha ha. . .!

MONSIEUR JOURDAIN Straighten the rooms and —

NICOLE Ha ha ha. . . Look, master, the best thing is — let me laugh all I want, then hit me. . . Ha ha ha. . .!

MONSIEUR JOURDAIN I'm burning.

NICOLE Please, master, let me laugh it out . . . Ha ha ha!

MONSIEUR JOURDAIN If I catch you laughing or even —

NICOLE Ma-ha-ha-haster, I'll explo-ho-ho-hode if I don't la-ha-ha-haugh.

MONSIEUR JOURDAIN Such brass! I'm giving her instructions and she laughs them back in my teeth.

NICOLE What do you have for me to do?

MONSIEUR JOURDAIN Put my house in order for the company we're expecting shortly.

NICOLE You've cured me. I don't feel like laughing any more. We get in such a mess here when you have company. That word company's enough to put me in a bad mood.

MONSIEUR JOURDAIN And so? Am I supposed, for your sake, to shut everybody out?

NICOLE Shut some people out, anyway.

Enter Madame Jourdain.

MONSIEUR JOURDAIN Aha, here's another novelty. What are you up to, husband, flying the colors? You want everyone to jeer at you?

MONSIEUR JOURDAIN The only ones who will jeer, woman, are the fools — of both sexes.

MADAME JOURDAIN Everyone's been laughing at your antics for ages.

MONSIEUR JOURDAIN Kindly tell me, who is this "everyone?"

MADAME JOURDAIN People in their right minds. Me, I'm sick of the way you carry on. I don't recognize the house lately. It's Mardi Gras every day, nonstop, starting at daybreak. What with the din of fiddlers and singers, the whole neighborhood's up.

NICOLE The mistress said it. I wouldn't know how to keep the place clean with that crowd you invite in. Their shoes go all over town looking for mud to bring back here. Poor Françoise is just about frazzled polishing all that crud off the floors from your fine friends.

MONSIEUR JOURDAIN For a peasant girl, you have too big a mouth.

MADAME JOURDAIN Nicole's right. I'd like to know what you think you're up to at your age with a dance teacher.

NICOLE And that great lunk of a swordfighter who stomps in here, rocking the walls and dislodging half the tiles.

MONSIEUR JOURDAIN Girl, woman: shut up!

MADAME JOURDAIN By the time you learn to dance your legs'll be shot, no?

NICOLE With a sword you can kill somebody, no?

MONSIEUR JOURDAIN Shut up, I said. You're both noneducated. You don't understand the amplications of all this.

MADAME JOURDAIN   You ought to be thinking, instead, about a husband for your daughter. She's coming of age.

MONSIEUR JOURDAIN   I'll think about Lucile's husband when the right one turns up. I'm trying to fix my mind on the higher things.

NICOLE   I heard, madame, that this morning, to cap it all, he took on a teacher of philosophy.

MONSIEUR JOURDAIN   . So I did. I'm out to get some culture and hold my own in intelligent company.

MADAME JOURDAIN   Maybe you'll go back to school one of these days so they can whip it into you.

MONSIEUR JOURDAIN   I swear to God I'd face a whipping here and now, in front of you all, if I could learn everything they teach in school.

MADAME JOURDAIN   You need all this nonsense to run a house.

MONSIEUR JOURDAIN   So I do. The two of you make me blush with your ignorance. For instance, do you know what you're talking?

MADAME JOURDAIN   Yes. I'm talking good sense and telling you to hurry up and change your ways.

MONSIEUR JOURDAIN   I don't mean that. I'm asking, what are these words you're speaking?

MADAME JOURDAIN   Words of commonsense, not like your actions.

MONSIEUR JOURDAIN   I said I don't mean that. What I'm saying to you, what I'm talking this minute — what is it?

MADAME JOURDAIN   Garbage.

MONSIEUR JOURDAIN   Will you listen? The language we're uttering.

MADAME JOURDAIN   So?

MONSIEUR JOURDAIN   You're unliterate. It's called prose.

MADAME JOURDAIN   Prose?

MONSIEUR JOURDAIN   Prose, yes. Whatever's prose is never verse and whatever's never prose can't be verse. That's how much studying can improve you. And you, Nicole, do you know how to make a U?

NICOLE   A what?

MONSIEUR JOURDAIN   Say U. See for yourself.

NICOLE   All right. U.

MONSIEUR JOURDAIN   What did you do?

NICOLE   I said U.

MONSIEUR JOURDAIN   Fine, but when you say U, what are you doing?

NICOLE   What you tell me.

MONSIEUR JOURDAIN   It's a wicked business trying to enlighten simpletons. Look, you push out your lips and bring the upper jaw down from the lower one. See that? U. I'm sulking. U.

NICOLE   Yes, that's sweet.

MADAME JOURDAIN   It's something to admire.

MONSIEUR JOURDAIN   It's a lot different when you come to O and Da da and Fa fa.

MADAME JOURDAIN   What is all this hocus-pocus?

NICOLE   Will it shake off germs, get rid of the pox?

MADAME JOURDAIN   You ought to give all those people and all their trash the heave-ho.

NICOLE   Start with that hulking monster and his swords who clogs up my house with dirt.

MONSIEUR JOURDAIN   The fencing teacher really bothers you, eh? I'll teach you a little respect for him. *(He has the foils brought over and gives one to Nicole.)*   Grab that. Logical demonstration. The line of the trunk. All you do to attack in quart is that. And to attack in tierce, that. And you avoid getting killed. That's not worth learning? To fight someone and know you're safe? Go ahead, attack me. See for yourself.

NICOLE   Anything you say. Like this?

She lunges several times and hits him.

MONSIEUR JOURDAIN   Hey, ho, wait, stop! Damn the girl!

NICOLE   You told me to.

MONSIEUR JOURDAIN   Yes, but you're supposed to attack in tierce before you attack in quart. You didn't give me a chance to parry.

MADAME JOURDAIN
                My dear, you've lost your mind.
                You're living in a dream
                by mixing with these high-class types. . .

MONSIEUR JOURDAIN
                Cream of the cream of the cream.
                Now take the Count Dorante,
                he's friends with gentlefolk
                and mentions me in front of them!

MADAME JOURDAIN
                You stake him when he's broke.
                What does he pay you back?

MONSIEUR JOURDAIN
                His friendship, his panache.
                He knows the king, the queen, the court.

MADAME JOURDAIN
                I'd rather have the cash.

MONSIEUR JOURDAIN   Quiet, here he is.

MADAME JOURDAIN   That's all we needed. He's here, you can bet, for another loan. The sight of him turns my stomach.

MONSIEUR JOURDAIN   Quiet, I said!

Enter Dorante.

DORANTE   Jourdain, my dear friend, how do you do?

MONSIEUR JOURDAIN   Very well, monsieur, humbly at your service.

DORANTE   And your good wife there, how is she doing?

MADAME JOURDAIN   She's doing her best.

DORANTE   What's all this finery, Jourdain? Properly in the fashion, eh?

MONSIEUR JOURDAIN   Oh, you know. . .

DORANTE   You look dazzling in that suit. We haven't one person at Court better dressed than you.

MONSIEUR JOURDAIN   Hee hee.

MADAME JOURDAIN   *(To Nicole)*   Scratching him where he itches.

DORANTE   Turn around. Yes, that's quite, quite modish.

MADAME JOURDAIN   *(To Nicole)*   The back's as dumb as the front.

DORANTE   On my soul, Jourdain, I've been uncommonly eager to see you again. I think more highly of you than of anybody. Only this morning I spoke of you in the king's bedroom.

MONSIEUR JOURDAIN   I'm honored, monsieur. *(To Madame Jourdain)*   In the king's bedroom!

DORANTE   Come now, your hat. Back on with it!

MONSIEUR JOURDAIN   I must show my respect for you, monsieur.

DORANTE   Good heavens, put it on. Please let's have no ceremony between you and me.

MONSIEUR JOURDAIN   But monsieur —

DORANTE   I insist, Jourdain. Hat on! You're my friend.

MONSIEUR JOURDAIN   Monsieur, I'm your servant and —

DORANTE   I won't cover my head unless you do.   Immediately.

MONSIEUR JOURDAIN   *(Donning his hat)*   I'd rather be right than hesitant.

DORANTE   I'm in debt to you, as you know.

MADAME JOURDAIN   We know.

DORANTE   On occasion you've lent me money in the most gracious manner.

MONSIEUR JOURDAIN   Monsieur, you're exaggerating.

DORANTE   I came here expressly to even things up, to straighten out our account.

MONSIEUR JOURDAIN   *(To his wife)*   See? After all the fuss you made.

DORANTE   I like to shake free of encumbrances as soon as possible.

MONSIEUR JOURDAIN   *(To his wife)*   Didn't I tell you?

DORANTE   Let's calculate exactly what I owe you.

MONSIEUR JOURDAIN   *(To his wife)*   You and your suspicions — ridiculous.

DORANTE   Do you recall the total sum?

MONSIEUR JOURDAIN   I think I do. I made notes. Here they are. One was for two hundred louis.

DORANTE   So it was.

MONSIEUR JOURDAIN   Another time, six score.

DORANTE   Correct.

MONSIEUR JOURDAIN   And another time, one hundred forty.

DORANTE   Correct again.

MONSIEUR JOURDAIN   Those three items make four hundred sixty louis, that is, five thousand and sixty livres.

DORANTE   Perfect arithmetic. Five thousand and sixty livres.

MONSIEUR JOURDAIN   One thousand eight hundred thirty-two livres for the man who designs your plumes.

DORANTE   Yes.

MONSIEUR JOURDAIN   Two thousand seven hundred eighty livres for your tailor.

DORANTE   Just so.

MONSIEUR JOURDAIN   Four thousand three hundred seventy-nine livres, twelve sols and eight deniers for your harness-maker.

DORANTE   It all adds up. To how much?

MONSIEUR JOURDAIN   Grand total: fifteen thousand eight hundred livres.

[Note to directors and actors: It hardly matters whether a modern audience "gets" these sums when they are expressed in livres, louis, deniers, and other exotic, pre-metric coinages. The point is that large amounts changed hands. Converting these into dollars or pounds or even francs is likely to take some of the flavor — and mystery — out of the accounting. At that time the livre and the franc were the same; so were the pistole and the louis, each worth eleven livres. Tr.]

DORANTE   Wonderful: fifteen thousand eight hundred. Tack on the two hundred pistoles you're going to give me now, and we round the whole thing off to eighteen thousand livres. Which I will repay at the first opportunity.

MADAME JOURDAIN *(To her husband)* Ha! Did I guess or didn't I?

MONSIEUR JOURDAIN Hush!

DORANTE It won't put you out to let me have that much?

MONSIEUR JOURDAIN Put me out? Me!

MADAME JOURDAIN *(To her husband)* You're the cow; he's the milkmaid.

MONSIEUR JOURDAIN Quiet!

DORANTE If it does, I'll get it from somebody else.

MONSIEUR JOURDAIN Please, no, monsieur.

MADAME JOURDAIN *(To her husband)* He won't stop till you're wiped out.

MONSIEUR JOURDAIN *(To his wife)* Quack, quack, quack.

DORANTE Do let me know if it's awkward for you, Jourdain.

MONSIEUR JOURDAIN Not in the least.

MADAME JOURDAIN *(To her husband)* A leech, that's what he is.

MONSIEUR JOURDAIN *(To his wife)* That's enough from you.

MADAME JOURDAIN *(To her husband)* He'll bleed you out of your last sou.

MONSIEUR JOURDAIN *(To his wife)* Enough, I said.

DORANTE I know people galore who'd be delighted to help out. But you're my closest friend: I thought it would be unfair if I asked others.

MONSIEUR JOURDAIN You couldn't pay me a nicer compliment, monsieur. I'll bring it right away.

MADAME JOURDAIN *(To her husband)* I don't believe this.
You're not giving him more?

MONSIEUR JOURDAIN *(To his wife)* How can I say no? A
nobleman who spoke about me this morning in the king's bedroom?

MADAME JOURDAIN *(To her husband)* You're a royal pushover.

Exit Monsieur Jourdain.

DORANTE You look quite down in the mouth, Madame Jourdain.
Is anything wrong?

MADAME JOURDAIN My head's bigger than my fist. But not as
thick.

DORANTE I don't see your daughter. Where is she?

MADAME JOURDAIN Wherever she is, she's better off there.

DORANTE How is she getting along?

MADAME JOURDAIN On foot.

DORANTE Would the two of you care to see the ballet and theatre
when they play before the king?

MADAME JOURDAIN Oh yes, we could use a good laugh.

DORANTE I'll wager you had scores of admirers, Madame
Jourdain, when you were young, witty and attractive.

MADAME JOURDAIN Ah, poor old Madame Jourdain, she must be
on her last legs.

DORANTE I wasn't thinking. Please pardon the discourtesy. I'm
sometimes bemused. You're still fairly young, of course.

Re-enter Monsieur Jourdain.

MONSIEUR JOURDAIN Here we are. Exactly two hundred louis.

DORANTE Jourdain, I assure you I'm yours completely, and
longing to do something for you at court.

MONSIEUR JOURDAIN   I'm hopelessly obliged to you.

DORANTE   If your wife cares to sit in on the king's entertainment, I'll obtain the best seats.

MADAME JOURDAIN   Madame Jourdain would love to, some other year.

DORANTE   *(To Monsieur Jourdain)*   You saw my note?   Our lovely marquise will be here shortly.   I managed to induce her to attend your luncheon and ballet.

MONSIEUR JOURDAIN   Let's step over there, monsieur, out of the way, for obvious reasons.

DORANTE   Since I saw you last week I haven't told you about the diamond you gave me for her.   I had a terrible time bringing her around.   She couldn't make up her mind to accept it until this morning.

MONSIEUR JOURDAIN   Did she like it?

DORANTE   Loved it.   I'll be astonished if the beauty of that diamond doesn't give you a powerful hold on her affections.

MONSIEUR JOURDAIN   Please God!

MADAME JOURDAIN   *(To Nicole)*   Once he's with that scrounger, he can't shake him off.

DORANTE   I made sure she appreciated the value of the jewel and the depth of your passion.

MONSIEUR JOURDAIN   Your kindness overwhelms me, monsieur. I'm at a loss when a quality person like you stoops to put yourself out for me.

DORANTE   Please, Jourdain, no class barriers between friends, eh? You'd do as much for me if you had the chance.

MONSIEUR JOURDAIN   I would, I would, with all my heart.

MADAME JOURDAIN   *(To Nicole)*   I can't stand having him here.

DORANTE   When you confessed your love for the beautiful marquise, who's an acquaintance of mine, you saw how zealously I offered my assistance.

MONSIEUR JOURDAIN   That moved me, it really did. It still does.

MADAME JOURDAIN   *(To Nicole)*   He makes me gag. Isn't he ever going?

NICOLE   They're cozy together.

DORANTE   Women love to have money squandered on them. All those serenades you commissioned, your barrage of flowers, the magnificent fireworks over the water, the diamond you bestowed on her, and now the reception you're giving — as love tokens they're far more eloquent than any words you could speak.

MONSIEUR JOURDAIN   A lady like that attracts me so strongly I'd pay any price for the privilege.

MADAME JOURDAIN   Nicole, how can they have so much to say to each other? Slip over there and listen in.

DORANTE   Soon you'll have the pleasure of meeting her here in comfort and feasting your eyes on her.

MONSIEUR JOURDAIN   I've cleared the decks. My wife's eating lunch at my sister's and staying on there for the afternoon.

DORANTE   That was prudent. Your wife would have made things awkward for us. I gave the recipes and instructions to your cook and made the preparations for the ballet, which I choreographed myself. So long as the performance lives up to the inspiration, I'm convinced that it will be —

MONSIEUR JOURDAIN   *(Noticing Nicole nearby)*   What's this? *(He boxes her ears.)*   How dare you!   *(To Dorante)*   Let's continue outside, monsieur.

They leave.

NICOLE   Ow! I got more of an earful than I bargained for. I'd say they must be up to some shady business and they want to keep you out of it.

MADAME JOURDAIN Nicole, this isn't the first time I've been suspicious of my husband. Unless I'm wildly mistaken, there's some romance in the works, and I'm determined to find out more about it. But I must talk to you about my daughter. You know Cléonte's in love with her. I'm fond of that boy. I'd like to arrange for him and Lucile to marry.

NICOLE I'm so happy to hear you say that, madame. If you're fond of the master, I'm just as fond of his valet. I only wish we could hold our wedding in the shadow of theirs.

MADAME JOURDAIN Go bring Cléonte. I'll be waiting. The two of us can put the proposal to my husband.

NICOLE Delighted, madame. *(Exit Madame Jourdain.)* This ought to make the boys happy. *(Enter Cléonte and Covielle.)*   You're here — a lucky break! I have some great news for you. I —

CLEONTE Stay away from me, cheat. Don't try to pass off any more of your stories.

NICOLE Is this how you welcome my —

CLEONTE Away! Tell your deceitful mistress she'll never again make a fool of Cléonte.

NICOLE Are you coming down with something? Covielle dear, what's all this about?

COVIELLE Out of my sight, girl. Don't come near me again.

NICOLE You too? Starting this —?

COVIELLE Out, I said. Not another word from you — ever!

NICOLE Some new bug in the air? I'll tell the young mistress. . . *(Exit.)*

CLEONTE
        After the tender promises I swore. . .

COVIELLE
        After I helped her scrub the lower floor. . .

CLEONTE
>   After I deluged her with my devotion...

COVIELLE
>   After I gave her salts to ease her motion...

CLEONTE
>   How can I bear this sort of a betrayal?

COVIELLE
>   What! Let her get away with such a trick?
>   I ought to crown her with her kitchen pail.

CLEONTE
>   Give her a frown.

COVIELLE
>   A sock.

CLEONTE
>   A snub.

COVIELLE
>   A kick.

CLEONTE
>   Make me defeat her. Fan my righteous anger.
>   Draw me a portrait of her; set me straight
>   so that I long to torture her, to hang her.
>   Prove she's the woman I was born to hate.

COVIELLE
>   Well, she has really tiny eyes. They're flinty.

CLEONTE
>   Have you seen how they glow, so full of fire,
>   and sometimes smolder?

COVIELLE
>   No, I'd say they're squinty.
>   Her mouth's too big —

CLEONTE
>   That mouth inflames desire.

Kissable lips! They tempt you, melt you, burn you!

COVIELLE

As for her figure, keep it!   She's too short.

CLEONTE

Yes, but the shape of it's enough to turn you
'round in your tracks.

COVIELLE

And then she has that wart.

CLEONTE

That's not a wart. A mole!

COVIELLE

Her conversation
sounds like a squeaky door. Her voice is sharp.

CLEONTE

Yes, with a strange, hypnotic palpitation —
words in the ether, music from a harp. . .

COVIELLE

She's also solemn.

CLEONTE

What do you want her? Joking?
laughing and making cracks that are inane?
Doesn't it bore you, isn't it provoking
being with a girl who gurgles like a drain?

COVIELLE

Why do I waste my time? She's your ideal.

CLEONTE

How can I help it? That's the way I feel.
As the most tragic, sorrowful of men,
I'll die before I speak to her again.

COVIELLE Watch it. Here she comes.

Enter Lucile and Nicole.

NICOLE   Yes, it took me back.

LUCILE   I told you what must have caused it. Here he is.

CLEONTE   I won't speak to her.

COVIELLE   Nor will I.

LUCILE   What is it. Cléonte? Something the matter?

NICOLE   Covielle, what's *with* you?

LUCILE   Why are you angry?

NICOLE   How come all the sulks?

LUCILE   Cléonte, why don't you answer?

NICOLE   Covielle, you been struck dumb?

CLEONTE   It was treachery.

COVIELLE   Judas in skirts.

LUCILE   Are you offended because of our meeting today?

CLEONTE   They realize what they did.

NICOLE   When we gave you the cold shoulder, did we put your back up?

COVIELLE   Now they're turning the knife.

LUCILE   Isn't that the reason, Cléonte, for your pique?

CLEONTE   If I must answer, yes, it is. But I'll tell you now that when you turn me down you won't have the satisfaction you hoped for. I'll do it to you first. I'll steal the initiative. Perhaps I'll be miserable. I'll suffer for a while. But I'll recover, because I'd rather cut my heart open than come crawling back to you.

COVIELLE   Me too.

LUCILE   All this fuss over nothing. Cléonte, let me explain why I didn't acknowledge you this morning. . .

The two women are now pursuing the men around the stage.

CLEONTE   I don't want to hear.

NICOLE   Covielle, this is why we looked away . . .

COVIELLE   Don't want to know.

LUCILE   As I was telling you —

CLEONTE   I said, no.

NICOLE   But see, we —

COVIELLE   Nothing doing.

LUCILE   Listen —

CLEONTE   Save your breath.

NICOLE   Let me speak.

COVIELLE   I'm deaf.

LUCILE   Cléonte!

CLEONTE   Never.

NICOLE   Covielle!

COVIELLE   Nix.

LUCILE   Wait.

CLEONTE   Lies.

NICOLE   Stop.

COVIELLE   Nuts.

LUCILE   One second.

CLEONTE   Not one.

NICOLE   Calm down.

COVIELLE   Push off.

LUCILE   Two words!

CLEONTE   Too late.

NICOLE   One word.

COVIELLE   Yes. Finished.

LUCILE   So be it. Think what you want. Do as you please.

NICOLE   Stew in your own juice.

CLEONTE   All right. Explain. Why did you turn your heads away from us?

The pursuit now goes into reverse as the men follow the women.

LUCILE   I don't choose to say.

COVIELLE   What was it all about?

NICOLE   I don't feel like telling you.

CLEONTE   Answer.

LUCILE   I have no desire to.

COVIELLE   Let me know.

NICOLE   I'll let you boil.

CLEONTE   Please.

LUCILE   Not a hope.

COVIELLE   Be kind.

NICOLE   Not a prayer.

CLEONTE   I beg of you.

LUCILE   Leave me.

COVIELLE   Come on.

NICOLE   Shove off.

CLEONTE   Lucile!

LUCILE   No.

COVIELLE   Nicole!

NICOLE   Nix.

CLEONTE   In the name of heaven!

LUCILE   Don't want to.

COVIELLE   Say something.

NICOLE   Not a word.

CLEONTE   Enlighten me.

LUCILE   Not a chance.

COVIELLE   Make me feel better.

LUCILE   Feel worse!

CLEONTE   *(Leaving)* So be it. You don't care for me enough. Look on me for the last time, woman I once idolized. I leave for a distant place where I shall die of grief and love.

COVIELLE   With me in his tracks.

LUCILE   Cléonte.

NICOLE   Covielle.

CLEONTE   Yes?

COVIELLE   What is it?

LUCILE   Where are you going?

CLEONTE   Where I said.

COVIELLE   To die.

LUCILE   Not to die, Cléonte!

CLEONTE   Yes, cruel woman. It's your wish.

LUCILE   My wish? That you die?

CLEONTE   Your wish.

LUCILE   If you'd listened, I'd have explained. My old aunt was with us this morning when we passed you. She insists that a girl compromises her honor if she merely lets a man near her. The way she describes it, every man is the Tempter, and we must run from the mere sight of him.

NICOLE   That's all there is to it.

CLEONTE   Lucile, you're not deceiving me?

COVIELLE   Nicole, you're not pulling a fast one?

LUCILE   I've told you the truth.

NICOLE   So help me, God.

COVIELLE   *(To Cléonte)*   Do we bite? Swallow?

CLEONTE   Lucile!

COVIELLE   Nicole!

CLEONTE   How easily the ones we love persuade us . . .

COVIELLE   How greasily the she-devils soft-soap us . . .

Enter Madame Jourdain.

MADAME JOURDAIN Cléonte, I'm so glad to see you. My husband's coming. Seize the chance. Ask him about marrying Lucile.

CLEONTE   That suggestion, madame, is music to my ears and balm to my desires. *(Enter Monsieur Jourdain.)*   Monsieur, I have a request. Without more preamble, I ask you for the honor, the glorious favor, of becoming your son-in-law.

MONSIEUR JOURDAIN Before I reply, monsieur, kindly tell me if you're a gentleman.

CLEONTE   Monsieur, the word "gentleman" gets bandied around freely. As a title it costs nothing to pick up and wear, not one scruple. My own feelings on the subject are perhaps finicky. I believe it's cowardly to disguise our God-given birth, and hope to be taken for what we are not. I have six years of army service to my credit; and my income enables me to live at a comfortable, respectable level. But I will not give myself a false title. And therefore I am not a gentleman.

MONSIEUR JOURDAIN Shake hands, monsieur. My daughter is not for you.

CLEONTE What?

MONSIEUR JOURDAIN You're not a gentleman. You don't get my daughter.

MADAME JOURDAIN You and your gentleman. Did you and I spring from the rib of royalty?

MONSIEUR JOURDAIN Quiet, woman. I see where you're heading.

MADAME JOURDAIN Your father was a storekeeper, wasn't he, like mine?

MONSIEUR JOURDAIN A fit on the woman! She brings up the same thing time and time again. If your father was a storekeeper, too bad for him. Anybody who says the same about my father has picked up some false information.   All I have to say to you is: I am going to have a son-in-law who's a gentleman.

MADAME JOURDAIN Your daughter ought to have a husband who suits her. Better somebody without a title who's well off and attractive than a gentleman who's poor and repulsive.

NICOLE That's the truth. There's a gentleman in our village back home with a son who's the clumsiest, dumbest deadbeat I ever saw.

MONSIEUR JOURDAIN Enough out of you, you walking noise. I'm capable of providing for my daughter. All she's short of is a title. I'm going to make her a marquise.

MADAME JOURDAIN A marquise?

MONSIEUR JOURDAIN Yes, a marquise.

MADAME JOURDAIN God forbid!

MONSIEUR JOURDAIN I'm set on it.

MADAME JOURDAIN I'm set against it. Marry over your head and you'll be sorry. I don't want a son-in-law who tells my daughter her parents aren't good enough or grandchildren who are ashamed to call me grandmother. If my daughter came for a visit acting like a great lady and forgot to say hello to the neighbors, "Look at her," they'd say, "our marquise, with her airs and graces. She's Jourdain's daughter. She wasn't always that high in the world. Both her grandfathers sold cloth near St. Innocent's Gate in the outdoor market. They put away money for their children, which is probably costing them dear in the next world, because you don't get that rich by being honest." That's what they'd say, and I don't want any part of it. I'd like a man who's thankful to be married to my daughter, so that I can say to him, "Sit there, son. Join us for dinner."

MONSIEUR JOURDAIN There speaks a person who wants to stay low on the ladder. No more back-talk. My daughter's going to be a marquise. And if you keep crossing me up, I'll make her a duchess. *(Exit.)*

MADAME JOURDAIN Cléonte, don't give up yet. Come with me, Lucile, and tell your father right out that it's Cléonte or no one.

Exeunt Madame Jourdain, Lucile, and Nicole.

COVIELLE   You made a nice shambles out of that with your finicky feelings.

CLEONTE   I stand by my principles.

COVIELLE   Principles — when you're dealing with a man like him? He's a lunatic, couldn't you tell?

CLEONTE   You're right. But I didn't think I'd have to produce proofs of noble birth to qualify as the son-in-law of Monsieur Jourdain.

COVIELLE   Ha ha ha ha ha. . .!

CLEONTE   Why are you laughing?

COVIELLE   I just came up with a plan.

CLEONTE   For what?

COVIELLE   For you. I got the idea from a masquerade. I could work it out for some actors. I can find the people and costumes in no time.

CLEONTE   But tell me —

COVIELLE   I'll fill you in on everything. I'll even coach you. Let's go: he's coming back.

Exeunt Cléonte and Covielle.

Re-enter Monsieur Jourdain.

MONSIEUR JOURDAIN   To hell with them all. They can't fault me for a thing except my friendships with the quality. Ah, those people live for honor and culture. I'd give two fingers off this hand to have been born Monsieur le Comte or Monsieur le Marquis. *(First Lackey enters.)* Yes?

FIRST LACKEY   Monsieur le Comte is here, monsieur, and he's brought a lady.

MONSIEUR JOURDAIN   Oh God, I haven't finished giving my instructions. Show them in and tell 'em I'll be right back. *(Exit.)*

Enter Dorimène and Dorante.

DORIMENE Am I doing the correct thing, Dorante, letting you bring me here? I don't know a soul in this house.

DORANTE Where else, madame? You want to avoid scandal, and—

DORIMENE But you're doing too much for me. Every day I become more committed to you ...
> You're spoiling me, spoiling me.
> Your extravagant routines,
> spending beyond your means
> on serenades, parades, and things
> like ruby bracelets and diamond rings
> are spoiling me, foiling me ...
> I must declare
> it's most unfair
> how you're luring me into
> your matrimonial lair.

DORANTE Madame, to win you I'd give a palace, a mountain, the earth, the firmament, my birthright and reputation — Ah, here comes the master of the house.

Re-enter Monsieur Jourdain. After two bows of greeting, he finds himself too close to Dorimène.

MONSIEUR JOURDAIN Back up a bit, madame.

DORIMENE What?

MONSIEUR JOURDAIN One step back, please.

DORIMENE What for?

MONSIEUR JOURDAIN The third bow. Pull back.

DORANTE Jourdain knows his manners, madame.

MONSIEUR JOURDAIN Madame, it's a glorious opportunity for me to be fortunate enough to be so happy as to have the luck to have you have the kindness of according me this badge of honor in honoring me with the favor of your presence, and if I also had the

merit of meriting a merit like yours, and were heaven . . . in envy
of my good fortune . . . to grant me . . . the boon of finding
myself worthy of the, the . . .

DORANTE   Now, now, Jourdain, that'll do. Madame doesn't care
for lengthy compliments. Besides, she realizes you're a man of
wit. *(To Dorimène)* He's a regular bourgeois — rather ludicrous,
as you see, with his proprieties.

DORIMENE   I noticed.

DORANTE   Madame, this is my closest friend.

MONSIEUR JOURDAIN   You do me too much honor.

DORANTE   A society lion.

DORIMENE   He stands high in my esteem.

MONSIEUR JOURDAIN   I haven't done a blessed thing yet, madame,
to earn that height in your esteem.

DORANTE   *(Aside, to Monsieur Jourdain)*   Take care, above all, not
to mention the diamond you gave her.

MONSIEUR JOURDAIN   Can't I even ask how she likes it?

DORANTE   Avoid doing that at any cost. It would seem crude. Act
as if you were not the one who gave it. *(Aloud)* Madame,
Jourdain says he's enchanted to see you in his house.

DORIMENE   He does me a great kindness.

DORANTE   *(To Monsieur Jourdain)*   I had a brutally difficult time
persuading her to come.

MONSIEUR JOURDAIN   I don't know how to thank you.

DORANTE   Madame, he says he finds you the loveliest of women.

DORIMENE   That's exceedingly gracious of him.

MONSIEUR JOURDAIN   You're the gracious one, madame, and —

DORANTE   We should think about lunch.

FIRST LACKEY   It's all ready, monsieur.

DORANTE   Let's take our seats. And send in the singers.

The Cooks, who have prepared the meal, put on a dance, which forms the third interlude and the end of the third act, after which they bring on a table set with dishes.

Intermission

PART TWO

Dorimène, Dorante, Monsieur Jourdain, Singers and Lackeys.

DORIMENE   Dorante! But this is a magnificent spread.

MONSIEUR JOURDAIN   You're teasing, madame, aren't you? I only
wish it was less unworthy of you.

They take their places at the table.

DORANTE   Jourdain is right, madame. I feel an obligation to him
for so warmly doing you the honors of his house. Still, I agree with
him. I ordered the meal myself but, unlike a certain society friend of
ours, I'm in the dark when it comes to the culinary arts. Now if that
friend had arranged for the meal, he'd rhapsodize over every course
laid before you. He'd speak of fresh bread, golden-crusted all over,
crumbling tenderly between your teeth; of the velvety strength of the
wine, young and fruity but not obtrusive; a shoulder of lamb
opulently garnished with parsley; Normandy veal, a loin this long,
white and delicate, as soft to the palate as almond paste; partridges
with a surprising fragrance of spices; and for his masterpiece, a
pearl-tinted broth inhabited by a fat young turkey flanked by squabs
and crowned with a marriage of white onions and chicory. But I
know nothing of all this. And as Jourdain so aptly remarks, I wish
the meal were less unworthy of you.

DORIMENE   I will answer that compliment by eating eagerly.

MONSIEUR JOURDAIN   Ah, beautiful hands!

DORIMENE   They're ordinary hands, Jourdain, but you may be
speaking of the diamond, which is indeed out of the ordinary.

MONSIEUR JOURDAIN   Not me, madame. God forbid that I say a
thing about it. That wouldn't be acting the gentleman. No, the
diamond isn't much.

DORIMENE   You're quite choosy.

MONSIEUR JOURDAIN   Thanks for saying so.

DORANTE   Come, another glass of wine for Jourdain, and some for our singers, who are going to give us a tribute to drinking.

DORIMENE   Music adds a marvelous seasoning to good food and wine. I am being so richly feasted!

MONSIEUR JOURDAIN   Oh, I wouldn't say —

DORANTE   Now, now, Jourdain, let's lend the singers our silence. Their voices will convey more than ours can.

First Drinking Song

SINGERS
> You and I and one glass of wine:
> I kiss your fingers and pass the wine.
> It wets your lips and again is mine . . .
> Drink, drink, my darling!
> You and I in a night of love:
> Our wine is full of the light of love.
> We three will climb to the height of love . . .
> Drink, drink, my darling!

Second Drinking Song, a Round

SINGERS
> If men must die, hooray, hooray,
> and time must fly, hooray,
> and fortune tellers lie, hooray,
> we'll sit and look up at the sky, hooray,
> and drink the night away, hooray,
> and maybe drink the day. . .

DORIMENE   I can't imagine better singing. That was beautiful.

MONSIEUR JOURDAIN   I see something even more beautiful here, madame.

DORIMENE   Well, well, Jourdain is even more gallant than I expected.

DORANTE   Truly, madame? What do you take him for?

MONSIEUR JOURDAIN   I know what I'd like her to take me for.

DORIMENE   Again?

DORANTE   You don't know him.

MONSIEUR JOURDAIN   She can know me any time she wants.

DORIMENE   I pass.

DORANTE   He's always quick with an answer. But you haven't observed, madame, that Jourdain eats every piece you touch.

DORIMENE   Jourdain is a fascinating man.

MONSIEUR JOURDAIN   If I could only fascinate you enough to —

Enter Madame Jourdain.

MADAME JOURDAIN   Aha, I see we have fine company. And I wasn't expected. So, my gentleman spouse, this party's why you packed me off to my sister-in-law's for a long lunch. Downstairs I noticed quite a performance getting under way, and up here I find something like a wedding banquet. This is how you play the host at home, is it? You treat ladies to music, a show, and a feast, while you send me out for some air.

DORANTE   What are these fantasies about your husband spending his money and giving the reception for this lady? I'm responsible, if you don't mind. He's done nothing more than lend me his house.

MONSIEUR JOURDAIN   The nerve of her! It's a fact: Monsieur le Comte is doing all this for madame, who's a lady of quality. He did me the favor of borrowing the house, and then asked me to join him.

MADAME JOURDAIN   Hokum. I know what I know.

DORANTE   Put on your glasses. Put them on!

MADAME JOURDAIN   I don't need any glasses. I could sense things, I could, and further back than yesterday. I'm not naive. It's sheer wickedness on your part, monsieur, a nobleman like you, to lend my husband a hand with his idiotic behavior. As for you, madame, it's not fair and not proper for a highborn lady like you to make trouble between a man and wife and let him get a crush on you.

DORIMENE What is all this about? Dorante, is this your idea of fun — to expose me to the ravings of this eccentric woman? *(Exit.)*

DORANTE Wait, madame! Madame, where are you off to? *(Exit.)*

MONSIEUR JOURDAIN Madame! Monsieur le Comte, apologize for me. Try to bring her back. You, woman! Now see what you've done. You walk in here, you insult me in front of everybody, and you hound the quality away from my house.

MADAME JOURDAIN Don't make me laugh. Quality!

MONSIEUR JOURDAIN I don't know what stops me from busting your head open with the plates from this meal you just ruined.

The lackeys take out the table.

MADAME JOURDAIN As if I care! I'm defending my rights, and all the women will support me. *(Exit.)*

MONSIEUR JOURDAIN She walked in at exactly the wrong moment. I was in the mood. I never felt more brilliant. *(Enter Covielle, disguised by a long, white beard.)* What on earth is this?

COVIELLE Monsieur, I don't believe I have the honor of being known to you.

MONSIEUR JOURDAIN No, monsieur.

COVIELLE When I first saw you, you were no bigger than that.

MONSIEUR JOURDAIN I was?

COVIELLE You were the most beautiful baby. The ladies used to take you in their arms and kiss you.

MONSIEUR JOURDAIN Real ladies? Kiss me?

COVIELLE Yes. I was a friend of your revered father.

MONSIEUR JOURDAIN   My revered father!

COVIELLE   Yes . . .
            Your father was a gentleman.

MONSIEUR JOURDAIN
            My father was . . .?

COVIELLE
            A gentleman!

MONSIEUR JOURDAIN
            You knew him as . . .?

COVIELLE
            A gentleman —
            a gentle, generous gentleman.

MONSIEUR JOURDAIN
            Some people say he bought and sold
            all sorts of vulgar merchandise
            and gloried in his hoard of gold.

COVIELLE
            A pack of lies, a stack of lies!
            Your father was a gentleman.

MONSIEUR JOURDAIN
            You promise now?

COVIELLE
            A gentleman!

MONSIEUR JOURDAIN
            You'll take a vow?

COVIELLE
            A gentleman,
            a gentle, generous gentleman.
            It's true he was a connoisseur
            of silk and wool and fine brocades,
            and strictly as an amateur,
            who knew his curtains, drapes, and shades,
            he sometimes picked out styles or blends

that followed all the latest trends
and bringing home these bolts and ends
he kindly gave them to his friends
for money. What a gentleman!
I take my oath, a gentleman.

MONSIEUR JOURDAIN
God save us both! A gentleman?

COVIELLE
A genuine, gentleman's gentleman.

Envoi

TOGETHER
Not a merchant with the poor joie-
de-vivre of a bourgeois,
a hummock of a stomach
and a mercenary mind —
But a gentleman
of the most
gentlemanly kind.

COVIELLE Yes, I've been traveling all over the world. I returned from my voyages only a few days ago. And because of my lasting interest in your family, I've come with some news that will thrill you.

MONSIEUR JOURDAIN I can't wait to hear.

COVIELLE The son of the sultan is here from Turkey.

MONSIEUR JOURDAIN The son of the sultan?

COVIELLE He's been received like visiting royalty. Which he is.

MONSIEUR JOURDAIN Strange. Nobody told me.

COVIELLE All the quality people want to meet him. But he — he is in love with your daughter.

MONSIEUR JOURDAIN The son of the sultan is?

COVIELLE That's right. He wants to be your son-in-law.

MONSIEUR JOURDAIN   The son of the sultan, my son-in-law?

COVIELLE   Your son-in-law, the son of the sultan. I went to see him. I'm fluent in the language, and we chatted. During the conversation, he said, "Acciam croc soler ouch alla moustaph gidelum, amanahem varahini oussere carbulath," which means, "Have you ever met that beautiful young lady who is the daughter of Monsieur Jourdain, a gentleman of Paris?"

MONSIEUR JOURDAIN   The sultan's son said that about me?

COVIELLE   Yes, and when I told him I knew you and I'd seen your daughter, "Aha," says he to me, "marababa sahem," meaning, "Oh, how I love her!"

MONSIEUR JOURDAIN   "Marababa sahem" means "Oh, how I love her!"

COVIELLE   Correct.

MONSIEUR JOURDAIN   I'm glad you let me in on that. I'd never have thought "Marababa sahem" could mean "Oh, how I love her!" It's a clever tongue, that Turkish.

COVIELLE   Cleverer than you'd imagine. Do you know the meaning of "cacaracamouchen?"

MONSIEUR JOURDAIN   Cacaracamouchen? No.

COVIELLE   "Cacaracamouchen" means "beloved."

MONSIEUR JOURDAIN   Beloved? Cacaracamouchen?

COVIELLE   Yes.

MONSIEUR JOURDAIN   That's a miracle. Cacaracamouchen, beloved! Who'd have guessed? That knocks me out.

COVIELLE   Now, as his acting ambassador, I have to announce that he wants to marry your daughter. But the father-in-law of the son of the sultan must hold a lofty title, and so he's going to appoint you a mamamouchi, which is a high dignitary in his country.

MONSIEUR JOURDAIN   Mamamouchi?

COVIELLE An authentic mamamouchi. In other words, what we call a paladin. A paladin is one of the ancient . . . paladins. It's among the noblest titles there is, and you'll be up there on a par with the greatest lords on earth.

MONSIEUR JOURDAIN This is a terrific privilege. Would you please take me to the son of the sultan so I can thank him?

COVIELLE No need to. He's on his way here.

MONSIEUR JOURDAIN Here? This house?

COVIELLE Yes, and he's bringing everything for your mamamouchi ceremony.

MONSIEUR JOURDAIN This is rather sudden.

COVIELLE He's so much in love, he can't wait.

MONSIEUR JOURDAIN There's one thing that makes me uneasy. My daughter's stubborn, and she's set her sights on a fellow named Cléonte. She swears it's Cléonte or nobody.

COVIELLE Wait till she meets the son of the sultan. She'll change her mind. By coincidence he looks very much like this Cléonte — I just saw the man; someone pointed him out to me. Her love for him could easily switch to the son of — I hear him coming. He's here.

Enter Cléonte in Turkish garb, attended by Pages.

CLEONTE Ambousahim oqui boraf, Iordina salamalequi.

COVIELLE That means, "May the heart of Jourdain flower all year like a rose bush." It's typical of their polite speech in those countries.

MONSIEUR JOURDAIN I'm the most humble servant of his Turkish highness.

COVIELLE Carigar camboto oustin moraf.

CLEONTE Oustin yoc catamalequi basum base alla moran.

COVIELLE He says, "May heaven bless you with the strength of bulls and the cunning of serpents."

MONSIEUR JOURDAIN Tell his Turkishness I wish him all the luck in the world.

COVIELLE Ossa binamen sadoc babally oracaf ouram.

CLEONTE Bel men.

COVIELLE He asks you to go with him right away to prepare for the ceremony, and then see your daughter, and conclude the marriage.

MONSIEUR JOURDAIN All that in two words?

COVIELLE That's what Turkish is like. In a couple of words you can say plenty. Go where he wants, now. *(Monsieur Jourdain follows Cléonte out.)* Ha ha ha ha. We're moving along. What a pawn! If he'd learned his lines by heart he couldn't play the part better. *(Enter Dorante.)* Monsieur, can I count on you to back our plan?

DORANTE Why, it's Covielle. Who'd know it? A transformation!

COVIELLE Certainly is. Ha ha ha ha ha. . .

DORANTE What are you laughing at?

COVIELLE Look at this get-up of mine. See if you can figure out our scheme to get Monsieur Jourdain to marry his daughter to my master?

DORANTE That I'd never guess. But I can guess that if you're behind it, it will work.

COVIELLE You know your fox.

DORANTE What are you up to?

COVIELLE A surprise. Step back here, if you will, and make room for some entertainment that's coming in.

The Fourth Interlude consists of a "Turkish" ceremony of music and dance, during which the bourgeois Monsieur Jourdain is ennobled.

Six Turks enter in pairs, dancing solemnly to the accompaniment of instruments. They carry three very long carpets with which they execute dance movements. At the end of this first episode they raise the carpets over their heads and Turkish Musicians and other Instrumentalists troop through underneath. To complete this march-dance, four Dervishes escort the Mufti into view.

The Turks lay their carpets on the ground and kneel on them. The Mufti stands in the center. Contorting his body and grimacing, he offers an invocation. He gazes upward and flaps his arms like wings. The Turks prostrate themselves as they chant "Ali" [the name of Mahomet's son-in-law]. They rise chanting "Allah," alternating the two names and the kneeling and rising, until the end of the invocation, when they all stand to chant, "Allah ekber {Great is God}."

The Dervishes lead in Monsieur Jourdain, who is dressed as a Turk, but shaven, without turban or scimitar. They present him to the Mufti, who gravely chants these words:

MUFTI

    If you know,
    say so.
    If you know not,
    say naught.
    Mufti am I,
    very high.
    You understand not?
    Say naught.   *(The Dervishes lead Monsieur Jourdain away.)*
    Answer, Turks, is this man a
    true believer? Or an Ana-
    baptist?

TURKS

    No.

MUFTI

    A Zwinglist?

TURKS

>No.

MUFTI

>A Copt?

TURKS

>No.

MUFTI

>A Hussite?
>A true-sight?
>Or an askew-sight?

TURKS

>No, no, no.

MUFTI

>No, no, no.
>Is he in truth a
>follower of Luther?

TURKS

>No.

MUFTI

>Hindu?

TURKS

>No.

MUFTI

>Shinto?

TURKS

>No.

MUFTI

>Faithless atheist?

TURKS

>No, no, no.

MUFTI

>No, no, no.
>Is he then Mahometan?
>Is he then Mahometan?

TURKS

>Hey valla!
>Yes, by Allah!

MUFTI

>What his name? What his name?

TURKS

>Jourdaina, Jourdaina.

MUFTI

>Jordaina. *(Whirling, looking around)* Jourdaina?
>Jourdaina?

TURKS

>Jourdaina, Jourdaina, Jourdaina!

MUFTI

>To Mahomet night and day
>for Jourdaina I will pray.
>Of Jourdaina, of Jourdaina
>I will make a paladaina.
>Give him turban, give him scimitar,
>give him galley to go on pilgrimitar.
>In his Turkish brigantina
>he will conquer Palestina.
>For Jourdaina night and day
>to Mahomet I will pray.
>Is he faithful Turk, Jourdaina?
>Is he faithful Turk, Jourdaina?

TURKS

>Hey valla!
>Yes, by Allah!
>Yes, by Allah!
>Hey valla!

MUFTI *(Dancing)*

>Hu la ba ba la chou ba la ba ba la da. *(Exit.)*

TURKS   *(Dancing)*
    Hu la ba ba la chou ba la ba ba la da.

*The Mufti re-enters wearing an enormous ceremonial turban with
four or five rows of lighted candles on top. Two Dervishes escort
him. They wear pointed hats also decorated with lighted candles.
They carry the Koran. Two other Dervishes bring in Monsieur
Jourdain, who is fearful about the ceremony. They make him
kneel, his back to the Mufti. Then forcing him to lean forward on
his hands, they place the Koran on his back to serve as the Mufti's
lectern.*

*The Mufti burlesques another invocation, frowning and opening his
mouth without making a sound. He pretends to declaim
vehemently, or he lowers his voice, or he shouts with trembling
excitement, or he pumps his body with his hands as if to drive out
the words, sometimes striking the Koran or riffling its pages.
Finally he raises his arms and shouts aloud, 'Hou," meaning "He!"
[Allah].*

*During this invocation the Turks chant, "Hou, hou, hou," bowing
each time, then chant "Hou, hou, hou," as they straighten up. They
continue this alternation until the Mufti's invocation is over.*

*The Dervishes remove the Koran. The Turks help Monsieur
Jourdain to his feet. As he stands up, stiff from holding the
posture, he lets out an "Oof!"*

MUFTI   *(To Monsieur Jourdain)*
    You no knave?

TURKS
    No, no, no.

MUFTI
    You no slave?

TURKS
    No, no, no.

MUFTI
    Give him turban, give him turban!

The Turks take off the Mufti's turban. He goes out.

TURKS

> You no knave?
> No, no, no.
> You no slave?
> No, no, no.
> Give him turban, give him turban!

The Turks dance and sing while they put the turban on Monsieur Jourdain.

The Mufti returns and hands Monsieur Jourdain a scimitar.

MUFTI

> Take this scimitar, let none deny
> you now noble, higher than I.   *(Exit.)*

TURKS

> Take this scimitar, let none deny
> you now noble, higher than I.

As they chant, six of the Turks, holding their scimitars, dance around Monsieur Jourdain and pretend to strike him. Re-enter the Mufti.

MUFTI

> Dara, dara, bastonara, bastonara, bastonara.
> Beat him, beat him, give him beating,
> give him beating, no retreating.   *(Exit.)*

TURKS   *(Tapping Monsieur Jourdain with their scimitars)*
> Give him beating, give him beating,
> thus completing all ill-treating.

MUFTI   *(Reappearing)*
> No ill-treating, no repeating,
> this has been the final beating.

TURKS

> No ill-treating, no repeating,
> this has been the final beating.

*The Mufti and Monsieur Jourdain are conducted offstage by the
Turks and the Dervishes to a musical accompaniment.*

[THIS IS THE END OF ACT FOUR.]

Enter Madame Jourdain.

MADAME JOURDAIN   Lord help me!   You look such a fright.   Who
fixed you up with that outfit?

MONSIEUR JOURDAIN   The gall of her, speaking that way to a
mamamouchi!

MADAME JOURDAIN   A mama what?

MONSIEUR JOURDAIN   From now on you'd better show me plenty
of respect.   They made me a mamamouchi.

MADAME JOURDAIN   Is that some creature?

MONSIEUR JOURDAIN   Mamamouchi.   A paladin.   That's me in
Turkish.

MADAME JOURDAIN   A turkey?

MONSIEUR JOURDAIN   Talk about ignorance!   I'm a dignitary now,
higher than a Mufti.   They had a ceremony for me.

MADAME JOURDAIN   What ceremony?

MONSIEUR JOURDAIN   To Mahomet night and day for Jourdaina I
will pray.

MADAME JOURDAIN   I don't get it.

MONSIEUR JOURDAIN   Jourdaina, that's Jourdain.

MADAME JOURDAIN   So it's Jourdain.   Then what?

MONSIEUR JOURDAIN   Of Jourdaina, of Jourdaina, I will make a
paladaina.

MADAME JOURDAIN   How?

MONSIEUR JOURDAIN Give him turban, give him scimitar.

MADAME JOURDAIN What for?

MONSIEUR JOURDAIN He will conquer Palestimita.

MADAME JOURDAIN What are you raving about?

MONSIEUR JOURDAIN Dara dara bastonara.

MADAME JOURDAIN Is that supposed to say something?

MONSIEUR JOURDAIN No ill-treating, no repeating, this has been the final beating.

MADAME JOURDAIN Final what?

MONSIEUR JOURDAIN Hou la ba ba la chou ba la ba ba la da.

MADAME JOURDAIN Come here, somebody! My husband's off his chump!

MONSIEUR JOURDAIN Peace, insolent woman! Show respect for the high and mighty mamamouchi! *(Exit.)*

MADAME JOURDAIN What happened to him? I'd better stop him from getting out. Who's coming? Those two again! This is the last straw plus one. Trouble, trouble on every side. *(She runs out.)*

Enter Dorimène and Dorante.

DORANTE Madame, we must do what we can for Cléonte and the girl by helping out with this masquerade. He's a well-bred youngster. We should show an interest in him.

DORIMENE Very well. But I must put an end to all this squandering, Dorante. I've made up my mind to marry you promptly. It seems the only answer. Marriage soon brings that sort of extravagance to a halt.

DORANTE Have you really decided —?

DORIMENE Only to save you from ruin. But here's our friend. He does look picturesque.

Enter Monsieur Jourdain.

DORANTE Madame and I are here, your excellency, to pay homage
to your new rank. And we rejoice with you in the marriage you've
made between your daughter and the son of the sultan.

MONSIEUR JOURDAIN *(After a Turkish bow)* Monsieur, I wish you
the strength of a snake and the cunning of a bull.

DORIMENE I'm glad to be among the first, your excellency, to
congratulate you on the awesome height you've risen to.

MONSIEUR JOURDAIN Madame, I hope your rosebush flowers all
year. I'm impossibly grateful to you for taking part in these honors
they're heaping on me. I also apologize diffusely for my wife's
outburst earlier.

DORIMENE I understand her feelings. She must be fearful about
holding on to the heart of a man like you.

MONSIEUR JOURDAIN My heart now belongs violently to you.

DORANTE There, madame. His excellency is not one of those people
blinded by good fortune. At the peak of his glory he still knows how
to acknowledge his friends.

DORIMENE That's the mark of a noble soul.

DORANTE But where's his Turkish highness? As your friends, we'd
like to pay our respects.

MONSIEUR JOURDAIN There he comes. I've sent for my daughter to
give her to him.

Enter Cléonte as the son of the sultan.

DORANTE Your highness, we come as friends of this gentleman,
your father-in-law, in order to —

MONSIEUR JOURDAIN Where's the interpreter to let him know who
you are? Wait till you hear 'em both talk Turkish. Fabulous!
Historic! Hey, where the devil's he got to? *(To Cléonte)* This
gentleman here's a bigwig, beeg weeg, a grande signore, grande
signore. And the lady's a granda dama, molto, molto special

dama granda. No get it? Him big mamamouchi français, French, see? And she lady mamamouchaise. I can't put it plainer. *(Enter Covielle.)* Where have you been? Look, tell him that monsieur and madame are quality people, will you, friends of mine. *(To Dorimène and Dorante)* Now watch. See how he answers.

COVIELLE Alabala crociam acci boram alabamen.

CLEONTE Catalequi tubal ourin soter amalouchan.

MONSIEUR JOURDAIN How about that?

COVIELLE He says, "May the rains of prosperity always water your family's garden."

MONSIEUR JOURDAIN See? What did I say? Real Turkish.

DORANTE Amazing.

Enter Lucile and Nicole.

MONSIEUR JOURDAIN Come along, my girl. Give your hand to the son of the sultan here.

LUCILE What's this, father? Dressed up in those things? Are you in a play?

MONSIEUR JOURDAIN Of course not. This is a serious business. Here's the husband I'm giving you.

LUCILE Giving *me?*

MONSIEUR JOURDAIN Go ahead. Let him take your hand, and thank God for your good luck.

LUCILE I've told you: I don't intend to marry.

MONSIEUR JOURDAIN Me, I intend it, and I'm your father.

LUCILE There's no power on earth that can make me take any man but Cléonte, and before I — *(Recognizing Cléonte)* before I say another word, I must remember that you're my father whom I will always obey.

MONSIEUR JOURDAIN My good girl! She knows her duty.

Enter Madame Jourdain.

MADAME JOURDAIN What's all this about? I hear you want to marry your daughter to a court jester.

MONSIEUR JOURDAIN Will you shut your face, woman? Your stupid discourtesies! I can't teach you to be reasonable.

MADAME JOURDAIN What's the crowd here for?

MONSIEUR JOURDAIN I'm marrying Lucile to the son of the sultan.

MADAME JOURDAIN The sultan's son?

MONSIEUR JOURDAIN The son of the sultan. Go over there and greet him through his interpreter.

MADAME JOURDAIN I'm not interested in his interpreter. I'll tell him to his face that he doesn't get my daughter.

DORANTE What's this, Madame Jourdain? You reject his Turkish highness as a son-in-law?

MADAME JOURDAIN Good God, monsieur, will you mind your own business?

DORIMENE It's a signal honor. Don't turn it down.

MADAME JOURDAIN You too, madame. Please don't interfere. This doesn't concern you.

DORANTE We are concerned. We're your friends.

MADAME JOURDAIN With friends like you . . .

DORANTE Your daughter there is willing to obey her father.

MADAME JOURDAIN What, and marry a Turk?

DORANTE Not just any Turk.

MADAME JOURDAIN She can forget Cléonte?

DORANTE What will a young woman not do to be a great lady?

MADAME JOURDAIN I'd strangle her with these hands.

LUCILE Mother . . .

MADAME JOURDAIN You! Away from me. You're bad.

MONSIEUR JOURDAIN Are you taking it out on her when she obeys me?

MADAME JOURDAIN She's mine as much as yours.

COVIELLE Madame . . .

MADAME JOURDAIN What do *you* want?

COVIELLE A word with you.

MADAME JOURDAIN Keep your word.

MONSIEUR JOURDAIN Listen to him, will you!

MADAME JOURDAIN I will not.

MONSIEUR JOURDAIN Is this an obstinate woman!

COVIELLE All you do is listen for a second. After that, it's up to you.

MADAME JOURDAIN I'll listen.

COVIELLE *(Aside, to her)* Don't you see? We're doing all this to play up to your husband's fantasy. We're in disguise to fool him. The son of the sultan is Cléonte.

MADAME JOURDAIN Oho!

COVIELLE And the interpreter, me, I'm Covielle.

MADAME JOURDAIN In that case, I give in.

COVIELLE Keep it quiet.

MADAME JOURDAIN *(To her husband)* I agree to the marriage.

MONSIEUR JOURDAIN At last! Everybody's reasonable.

MADAME JOURDAIN Let's send for a notary.

DORANTE That's the spirit. And now, Madame Jourdain, to relieve you of any further anxieties over your husband, this lady and I will employ the same notary for our marriage.

MADAME JOURDAIN I agree to that, too.

MONSIEUR JOURDAIN *(Aside, to Dorante)* Clever! That should convince her.

DORANTE Keep the secret. She'll never know.

MONSIEUR JOURDAIN Good, good. *(Aloud, to a Lackey)* You! Go out for a notary.

DORANTE While we're waiting for him, let's watch my ballet with his Turkish highness.

MONSIEUR JOURDAIN A very bright idea. Come, take our seats.

MADAME JOURDAIN What about Nicole?

MONSIEUR JOURDAIN I give her to the interpreter. And my wife to anyone who'll take her.

COVIELLE Monsieur, I thank you.
              (Aside) If you've ever heard of anyone more weird,
              tell me after the show and I'll eat my beard.

The play closes with The Ballet of the Nations *or with the opera* Ariadne auf Naxos *by Strauss and Hofmannsthal or without further ado.*

The end of
The Bourgeois Gentleman

POSTSCRIPT

Molière's earliest known skit on medicine occurs in his second play *The Flying Doctor,* portions of which appear with some dressing-up in two later plays, one being *The Doctor in Spite of Himself.* But Molière frequently (and sometimes bitterly) twitted the medical profession in other plays. Some critics trace the reason to his own infirmities, especially during his last years when medicine did not save him and when, at the age of 51, he knew himself to be a dying man. In her television series about the life of the playwright, Ariane Mnouchkine took his resentment back to the time when he watched his mother die at the hands of pretentious incompetents. But an author does not necessarily choose to write about what he hates, and may never get around to *everything* he hates if he is a good, comprehensive hater. Medical practices and malpractices are propitious material for the stage, and even more propitious for the legal profession today.

Bodily health, that ideal state that everybody aspires to, that mere absence of sickness, is a mysterious objective. There is no one way for everybody to catch it. Over the millennia and across the world it has been sought through the agencies of superstition and witchcraft and religious faith, as well as through the efforts of trained healers. It has provided a fine living for many a mercenary and charlatan. Some people want to be in that negative condition of health so fiercely, and have so little notion of what it might be, that to enjoy its theoretical benefits they will harken to any plausible tongue, any charm or spell. They will pay through the nose and subject themselves to periodic nuisance rituals — pill-popping, draining exertions, scalding baths, starvation, injections — in order to keep illness at bay. Their invalidism may turn into a hobby or become a badge of honor, something to brag about.

The older theories of medicine, in Molière's time, assumed that good health had to displace ill health, had to cast it out, much as one had to expel a demon or succubus in order to get rid of spiritual sickness. The commonest medicines were therefore enemas and laxatives. But the cleaning out might also take such other forms as the letting of "bad" blood. Even *l'or potable,* literally drinkable gold, which is alluded to in *The Doctor in Spite of Himself,* was revered as the most precious and expensive of substances which would in some fashion discharge all ills from the body and continue to ward them off. The craving for health, then, has dramatic potential. It implies unstable alliances between gullible, eager victims and ruthless, eager exploiters.

Like the patients and their caretakers in Molière's plays, many people today would like to believe that every ailment is curable. Medical mumbo-jumbo doesn't really persuade them; it only tames them for the moment. They have to wait and see. Medicated patients do occasionally get worse. They may die. Some recover in spite of medicine. Others, who ask for second or third opinions, may pay for opposed diagnoses and treatments. But they certainly pay. As with other professions, such as the law and income tax accounting, medicine charges for consultation, not for results.

Several characters in *The Doctor in Spite of Himself* speak in a rustic dialect in the French. Rather than following the examples of earlier translators, who have put these lines into regional American or British forms (hillbilly, Cockney, a species of Irish, and so on), which sounds literally out of place and is more often confusing than amusing (Lady Gregory's being a marvel of an exception), I have resorted to malapropisms, spoonerisms, and other inventions. This practice incurs more than one sort of distortion. It may mean substitution, rather than strict translation, and it loses some of the flair of the original, which gives us the same sort of pleasure we get listening to the dialect in Harold Pinter, David Mamet, and Amiri Baraka. However, the most precise version of Molière's 17th-century French doesn't recapture the flavor for modern English-speaking spectators. Vernacular speech is one of the translator's most trying puzzles. I have equally attempted to stay away from the excessively formal, sometimes stilted English usually associated with Molière in translation. To his original audiences his language sounded surprisingly modern because it had a natural ring to it that the writings of his contemporaries lacked.

In *The Bourgeois Gentleman* the alterations consist mostly of putting some of the lines into rhyming lyrics. There are songs in the French text, and the fourth act's mamamouchi-coronation of Monsieur Jourdain almost demands accompanying music. Jean-Louis Barrault's bold and virtually choreographic interpretation of the play in the early 1970s at the Comédie-Française went so far as to enlist the audience in singing refrains during that sequence.

Previous translations have been careful not to use the word *bourgeois* in the title, many preferring the compound adjective *would-be*. I prefer the original because of its ironic, almost oxymoronic character. American audiences who attended performances of this translation did not appear to be baffled by *bourgeois,* possibly because the dialogue makes amply clear the difference between a gentleman, a low-to-middling rank in the nobility, and a bourgeois, or member of the merchant class; and there seems to be no reason to shy away from a French word that English has gratefully adopted.

Albert Bermel
The Bronx, New York, 1987

THE MISANTHROPE
AND OTHER FRENCH CLASSICS

THE MISANTHROPE • Molière
PHAEDRA • Racine
THE CID • Corneille
FIGARO'S MARRIAGE • Beaumarchais
paper • ISBN: 0-936839-19-8

LIFE IS A DREAM
AND OTHER SPANISH CLASSICS

LIFE IS A DREAM • Calderon de la Barca
FUENTE OVEJUNA • Lope de Vega
THE TRICKSTER OF SEVILLE • Tirso de Molina
THE SIEGE OF NUMANTIA • Miguel de Cervantes

paper • ISBN: 1-55783-006-1   cloth • ISBN 1-55783-005-3

THE SERVANT OF TWO MASTERS
AND OTHER ITALIAN CLASSICS

THE SERVANT OF TWO MASTERS • Goldoni
THE KING STAG • Gozzi
THE MANDRAKE • Machiavelli
RUZZANTE RETURNS FROM THE WARS • Beolco
paper • ISBN: 0-936839-20-1

ERIC BENTLEY'S

❀**APPLAUSE**❀

THE MISER
and
GEORGE DANDIN
by Molière
Translated by Albert Bermel

Harpagon, the most desperate, scheming miser in literature, starves his servants, declines to pay them, cheats his own children if he can save (or make) a few coins, and when his hoard of gold disappears, insanely accuses himself of being the thief.

Dandin, in this rousing classic, not previously available in English for sixty years, is a man in a plight that everybody but him will find entertaining.

paper • ISBN: 0-936839-75-9

❦APPLAUSE❦

SCAPIN
and
DON JUAN
by Molière
Translated by Albert Bermel

In one of Molière's most popular plays, Scapin, that monarch of con men, puts his endless store of ingenuity to work, getting two lovesick young men married to the girls they pine for and, along the way, taking revenge on their grasping old fathers.

Closed down after its first, highly successful run because of opposition from powerful enemies of the playwright, *Don Juan* was performed in a bowdlerized version for almost two hundred years, until actors, directors and critics restored the original text, recognizing it as the most ambitious and mightiest of Molière's prose plays

paper • ISBN: 0-936839-80-5

❦APPLAUSE❦

TOUR DE FARCE SERIES
translated by Norman R. Shapiro

THE PREGNANT PAUSE or
LOVE'S LABOR LOST
by Georges Feydeau

Hector Ennepèque, first-time father-to-be, is in extended labor and protracted comic convulsions over his wife Léonie's imminent delivery. A brilliant tableau of conjugal chaos by the master of the genre.

paper • ISBN: 0-936839-58-9

A SLAP IN THE FARCE and
A MATTER OF WIFE AND DEATH
by Eugene Labiche

An accidental grope on a dimly lit bus earns for the painter, Antoine, a slap whose force resounds around Labiche's wildly comic labyrinth, from which there is no escape, except, alas, for (what else?) romance and marriage.

paper • ISBN: 0-936839-82-1

THE BRAZILIAN
by Henri Meilhac and Ludovic Halèvy

Two amorous actresses are out to capture the affections of a wealthy Paris producer. The play's mad improvisation is a romp in the best tradition of door-slamming French bedroom farce.

paper • ISBN: 0-936839-59-7

❧APPLAUSE❧

SOLILOQUY!
The Shakespeare Monologues
Edited by Michael Earley and Philippa Keil

At last, over 175 of Shakespeare's finest and most performable monologues taken from all 37 plays are here in two easy-to-use volumes (MEN and WOMEN). Selections travel the entire spectrum of the great dramatist's vision, from comedies and romances to tragedies, pathos and histories.

"SOLILOQUY *is an excellent and comprehensive collection of Shakespeare's speeches. Not only are the monologues wide-ranging and varied, but they are superbly annotated. Each volume is prefaced by an informative and reassuring introduction, which explains the signals and signposts by which Shakespeare helps the actor on his journey through the text. It includes a very good explanation of blank verse, with excellent examples of irregularities which are specifically related to character and acting intentions. These two books are a must for any actor in search of a 'classical' audition piece."*

ELIZABETH SMITH
Head of Voice & Speech
The Juilliard School

paper • MEN: ISBN 0-936839-78-3 • WOMEN: ISBN 0-936839-79-1

❦APPLAUSE❦

THE THREE CUCKOLDS
by Leon Katz

"They loved him in Venice and Rome, and Verona, and Padua. That was 400 years ago, but they also love him NOW! Arlecchino, chief clown and scapegoat of commedia dell'arte commedy makes a triumphal comeback in *The Three Cuckolds*!" —LOS ANGELES TIMES

paper • ISBN: 0-936839-06-6

THE SON OF ARLECCHINO
by Leon Katz

Watch out! CAUTION! Arlecchino and his band of madcaps are leaping out of centuries of retirement. They're fed up with being shoved around like second-rate citizens of the stage. Their revolt is led by none other than the champion of present day commedia, Leon Katz, who incites the troupe to perform all their most famous zany routines.

paper • ISBN: 0-936839-07-4

CELESTINA
by Fernando de Rojas
Adapted by Eric Bentley • Translated by James Mabbe

The central situation is a simple one: a dirty old woman is helping a courtly young gentleman to seduce a girl. The wonder of the thing lies in the art with which de Rojas derives a towering tragedy — or rather tragi-comedy.

paper • ISBN: 0-936839-01-5

♥APPLAUSE♥

MONOLOGUE WORKSHOP

From Search to Discovery
in Audition and Performance
by Jack Poggi

To those for whom the monologue has always been synonymous with terror, *The Monologue Workshop* will prove an indispensable ally. Jack Poggi's new book answers the long-felt need among actors for top-notch guidance in finding, rehearsing, and performing monologues. For those who find themselves groping for a speech just hours before their "big break," this book is their guide to salvation.

The Monologue Workshop supplies the tools to discover new pieces before they become over-familiar, excavate older material that has been neglected, and adapt material from non-dramatic sources (novels, short stories, letters, diaries, autobiographies, even newspaper columns). There are also chapters on writing original monologues and creating solo performances in the style of Lily Tomlin and Eric Bogosian.

Besides the wealth of practical advice he offers, Poggi transforms the monologue experience from a terrifying ordeal into an exhilarating opportunity. Jack Poggi, as many working actors will attest, is the actor's partner in a process they had always thought was without one.

paper • ISBN: 1-55783-031-2

❦APPLAUSE❦

CLASSICAL TRAGEDY
GREEK AND ROMAN: Eight Plays

In Authoritative Modern Translations
Accompanied by Critical Essays

Edited by Robert W. Corrigan

AESCHYLUS	**PROMETHEUS BOUND** translated by David Grene **ORESTEIA** translated by Tony Harrison
SOPHOCLES	**ANTIGONE** translated by Dudley Fitts and Robert Fitzgerald **OEDIPUS THE KING** translated by Kenneth Cavander
EURIPIDES	**MEDEA** translated by Michael Townsend **THE BAKKHAI** translated by Robert Bagg
SENECA	**OEDIPUS** translated by David Anthony Turner **MEDEA** translated by Frederick Ahl

paper • ISBN: 1-55783-046-0

❧APPLAUSE❧

CLASSICAL COMEDY
GREEK AND ROMAN: Six Plays
Edited by Robert W. Corrigan

The only book of its kind: for the first time Greek and
Roman masters of comedy meet in this extraordinary
new forum devised and edited by a master scholar of
comedy himself, Robert Corrigan. Corrigan has enlisted
six superb translations to create an unmatched Olympi-
ad of classical comedy.

ARISTOPHANES	**LYSISTRATA** translated by Donald Sutherland **THE BIRDS** translated by Walter Kerr
MENANDER	**THE GROUCH** translated by Sheila D'Atri
PLAUTUS	**THE MENAECHMI** translated by Palmer Bovie **THE HAUNTED HOUSE** translated by Palmer Bovie
TERENCE	**THE SELF-TORMENTOR** translated by Palmer Bovie

paper • ISBN: 0-936839-85-6

APPLAUSE

ON SINGING ONSTAGE
New, Completely Revised Edition
by David Craig

"*David Craig knows more about singing in the musical theatre than anyone in this country — which probably means in
the world. Time and time again his advice and training have
resulted in actors moving from non-musical theatre into musi-
cals with ease and expertise. Short of taking his classes, this
book is a must.*"

HAROLD PRINCE

In the New and Revised *On Singing Onstage* David
Craig presents the same technique he has given to Amer-
ica's leading actors, actresses and dancers over the past
thirty years. By listing the do's and don'ts of all aspects
of singing onstage, you will be brought closer to the discovery of your own personal "style." That achievement
plus information on how to get the most mileage out of
an audition (what to sing and how to choose it) makes
this book an indispensably practical self-teaching tool.

For anyone who has to (or wants to) sing anywhere,
from amateur productions to the Broadway stage, *On
Singing Onstage* is an essential guide for making the
most of your talent.

AMONG DAVID CRAIG'S STUDENTS:

*Carol Burnett, Cyd Charisse, James Coco, Sally Field, Lee
Grant, Valerie Harper, Barbara Harris, Rock Hudson, Sally
Kellerman, Jack Klugman, Cloris Leachman, Roddy
McDowell, Marsha Mason, Anthony Perkins, Lee Remick,
Eva Marie Saint, Marlo Thomas, Cicely Tyson, Nancy Walker
. . . and many more.*

paper • ISBN: 1-55783-043-6

❦**APPLAUSE**❦